knowledge management and information systems: strategies for growing organizations

knowledge management and information systems: strategies for growing organizations

Robert Mellor
Director of Enterprise,
Faculty of Computing, Information Systems and Mathematics
Kingston University

palgrave
macmillan

First published 2011 by
PALGRAVE MACMILLAN

Palgrave Macmillan in the UK is an imprint of Macmillan Publishers Limited, registered in England, company number 785998, of Houndmills, Basingstoke, Hampshire RG21 6XS.

Palgrave Macmillan in the US is a division of St Martin's Press LLC, 175 Fifth Avenue, New York, NY 10010.

Palgrave Macmillan is the global academic imprint of the above companies and has companies and representatives throughout the world.

Palgrave® and Macmillan® are registered trademarks in the United States, the United Kingdom, Europe and other countries.

ISBN: 978–0–230–28043–4

This book is printed on paper suitable for recycling and made from fully managed and sustained forest sources. Logging, pulping and manufacturing processes are expected to conform to the environmental regulations of the country of origin.

A catalogue record for this book is available from the British Library.

A catalog record for this book is available from the Library of Congress.

10 9 8 7 6 5 4 3 2 1
20 19 18 17 16 15 14 13 12 11

Printed and bound in Great Britain by
CPI Antony Rowe, Chippenham and Eastbourne

To my love and inspiration – Kate and Alice

contents

illustrations

figures

tables

this book: who is it for and what is it about?

Disordered knowledge is worthless. Winners like Google and Microsoft know that adding order to knowledge adds value, and this value can be used to further worthy ends. This book is essential reading for undergraduate and postgraduate students of all disciplines of business and management, as well as related disciplines like HRM, communications and production or operations management. Furthermore it provides the context for undergraduate students of computing and of Information Systems alike because it explains why you are studying what you are studying and by providing the framework, it will enable you to better choose your pathway of study. Subjects where this book is recommended reading include Strategic Innovation, eCommerce, Mobile Business, Entrepreneurial Management, Information Systems, Computer Science, Management Studies, Small Business Studies and a whole range of MBA topics.

Knowledge drives society. How can it be managed to profitably produce new services and innovations? This book uses Knowledge Valley Theory to put real financial values on knowledge plus illustrates how Web 2.0 technology can not only provide a cheap yet nimble platform for business processes but also inspire individuals and organizations to new heights. Leading expert in the field, Dr Rob Mellor, surveys the relevant background then shows in simple language how 'just-in-time' Information Systems can radically boost organizations, add resilience, sustain their growth and even calculate their return on investment.

about the author

Polyglot and polymath Robert B. Mellor is a Director of the Faculty of Computing, Information Systems and Mathematics at Kingston University, London where he lectures at postgraduate level on subjects like 'Strategic Information Systems', 'Knowledge Management', 'Strategic Innovation' and 'IT & Entrepreneurship'. He holds earned doctorates in various academic disciplines including innovation, computing and biology and is author of over 120 scientific publications in reputable journals, including e.g. 'Nature'. He has previously written ten books, including four on innovation and entrepreneurship. He is an active consultant with over twelve years industrial experience and has been expert advisor to several governments and the European Union since 1994.

disclaimer

Many software applications and systems, as well as websites, are mentioned in this work. These are meant purely as examples to illustrate the richness of the area. Inclusion here is by no means a recommendation for any of them (although many may be excellent) and conversely any exclusions are my ignorant omissions, with no slight intended. Furthermore the dynamic pace of software development and service delivery means that the area changes constantly and rapidly, so e.g. some applications deemed unsuitable for a particular task may have become suitable, while a suitable one may have been discontinued. At the end of the day any decision is the sole responsibility of the individual involved.

acknowledgements

I am grateful to the Oxford University Press for allowing me to draw on the works of Max Boisot and to the American Sociological Society for allowing me to draw on the works of James Davies.

preface

Paradigm changes and other forms of innovation drive the world forward and progress human knowledge and ability to new superior heights. Geopolitically, and especially relating to technological knowledge, the majority of the concepts and techniques come from the knowledge-intensive parts of the world commonly called 'the first world', but increasing globalization means that these can be copied – often in improved or cheaper forms – throughout the world and in ever-shorter cycles. This means that the rate of innovation in 'the first world' has to constantly increase in order to preserve a differential. At the moment it is not known if there is a theoretical threshold level of innovation, after which further innovation cannot be maintained and rates will level off, in a similar fashion to Moore's Law.[1] But what is apparent is that today's 'knowledge economy', Knowledge Management is even more relevant and economically important than ever before. However the context has changed from being a purely academic Business School subject (although 'real' scientists would perhaps balk at this description because proper control experiments are rarely performed) and applied mainly in large organizations. With the realization of the role of SMEs in national economy the new paradigm now includes innovation as a primary aim and then to strap this hybrid construction securely into a small enterprise and entrepreneurial framework.

The focus of this book is not primarily Knowledge Management in large organizations or Information Systems in large organizations. I will explain the reason for this apparently radical departure from Knowledge Management tradition as follows: Not only does the UK presently boast 3.5 million SMEs compared to some 7000 larger organizations, but also I believe that this trend will be followed by in other regions because small organizations can displace other small organizations by Darwinist competition at the marketplace, but as an industry matures a few giants will begin to dominate. In terms of Information Systems they will become tied down in their data structure – legacy systems are the death song of these dinosaurs. Being meritocratic I believe that everyone

---

[1] Gordon Moore's original statement is that the numbers of transistors in computers would double every year (he later revised that to every second year) and it can be found in an article entitled 'Cramming more components onto integrated circuits' published in the 19 April 1965 edition of *Electronics Magazine*. However in 2005 Moore stated in an interview that the law cannot be sustained indefinitely: 'It can't continue forever. The nature of exponentials is that you push them out and eventually disaster happens' and he noted that transistors would eventually reach their limits of miniaturization at atomic levels; 'We have another 10 to 20 years before we reach a fundamental limit' he is reported to have said (Dubash, 2005).

should get what they deserve and that dinosaurs deserve extinction. Most often, workers in Information Systems, upon being introduced to a large organization, will all too often first find a structure following departmental lines and political structures and secondly that any new additions to the systems are often first given for 'scoping' to expert consultants from competent and deservedly well-known firms like Accenture, CapGemmini, KPMG, Logica-FMG, McKinsey, PriceWaterhouseCoopers etc. to sculpture the specifications, with (understandably enough) little room is left over for spontaneity or manoeuvres. Thus the resulting vehicle of knowledge-sharing in a large organization then often becomes some kind of committee animal – often an intranet 'solution' and, even worse, the content may be maintained by the 'communications team', consisting of individuals of journalistic extraction (as rule of thumb 1 journalist per 500 productive employees) who can turn out handy short articles for popular consumption at short notice but hardly possess the background to be able to manage the hard and often technical knowledge at the required depth for changes in the structure of the core value chain, be it in product or process innovation, to occur. Certainly, one could argue the converse and point out that hard-working and charismatic leaders do appear occasionally and that they can indeed turn large organizations around. This is true and these phenomena are also given consideration towards the end of this book (Chapter 15).

Against this backdrop it can be seen that a proper field of endeavour for Knowledge Management specialists is in:

- giving guidelines for successfully growing new firms – as consultants or as entrepreneurs;
- for getting the knowledge structure (including the organizational culture) correctly placed as well as;
- getting correct and scalable Information Systems in place from the beginning.

Thus this book will feature SMEs – Small and Medium Sized Enterprises – also because this may be the type of environment where many business-oriented Information Systems analysts will work. One may justifiably ask; can these 'KM enabled' new small firms compete in the marketplace? The answer is ... perhaps!

Certainly many SMEs experience serious trouble upon rapid expansion, so getting correct and scalable Information Systems in place from the beginning (and for IT implementations that means correct, usable, scalable, flexible and – since it may well be trashed – with reusable components) will help. However prognostication is hard and foreseeing what the future holds for individuals or individual organizations is almost always impossible. But surely the overall aim of Knowledge Management is not so much to equip more firms to be able to better compete in the same marketplace as to enable them to innovate, to acquire or create new marketplaces and through this to eventually build whole new industries!

This book is structured to reflect this new concept: Chapters 1 to 5 inclusive provide a brief synopsis about the most important concepts in Knowledge Management, in Innovation, in Entrepreneurship and around SMEs respectively. These chapters thus provide a conceptual baseline upon which subsequent concepts are founded. Mathematical modelling has been performed on similar knowledge-related and organizational topics by Nissen (2008), Davis et al. (2007) and others and indeed following this tradition Chapter 6 introduces the simple basics used to construct the 3D fold called Knowledge Valley Theory (KVT) while Chapter 7 briefly places formal IPR in the valley. Chapters 8 and 9 simply add variables into the basic KVT model so some effects of overlapping knowledge (Chapter 8) and trust exclusion zones (Chapter 9) can be illustrated in a simple and understandable manner. Chapter 10 summarizes the points that KVT illustrates.

However, up to and including Chapter 9, KVT as presented has been based on certain stated assumptions. Chapter 11 revisits these assumptions and introduces the concept of weak ties being strong (Granovetter, 1973) and that Information Systems is not uniformly applicable to all subject matter and indeed also has weak and strong areas. The point is also made here that learning, e-learning and educational technologies – as a subset of Knowledge Management – belong at the 'back end' of the IT used in Information Systems. Chapter 12 sums up conclusions first in the light of Knowledge Management for business and business processes and then Chapter 13 examines the practical application of Information Systems technologies.

Being a practical exercise, as well as because we are dealing with a semi-quantitative model (i.e. KVT), Chapter 14 endeavours to put actual values (in money terms) on various Knowledge Management measures in general management terms. Chapter 15 then presents a rather open-ended speculation about how KVT could be expanded to encompass large organizations while all the literature cited is presented in the last section.

Finally it only remains for me to wish you good luck in your endeavours and I hope that your reading of this book will be as enjoyable for you, as writing it was for me.

1 general introduction

CTION TO INNOVATION • INTRODUCTION TO ENTREPRENEURSHIP • INTRODUCTION • CONSTRUCTING KNOWLEDGE VALLEY • MANAGING FORMAL KNOWLEDGE • USING KVT TO IDENTIFY INNOVATION BOOSTING FACTORS • FACTORS THAT STOP INNOVATION • A SUMMARY OF LESSONS LEARNT FROM KVT • RECOMBINING KNOWLEDGE AND LEARNING PROVOKES INSPIRATION • SOME CONCLUSIONS AND SUMMING UP • CHOOSING POSSIBLE TECHNOLOGIES • CALCULATE YOUR BENEFIT • LARGER ORGANIZATIONS

Among the theories presented and discussed in this book is Knowledge Valley Theory (KVT), a model based on simple mathematics which combines the field known as Knowledge Management with that called Innovation via the inter-linking discipline of Entrepreneurship. The business consequences of this new hypothesis are then viewed through the lens of Information Systems. Theories borrowed from both Education (pedagogy) and e-commerce will be used to cement the relationship with practical Information Systems. It may be surpris-ing to include e-commerce[1] here, but we are not talking about adWords on your intranet, rather that e-commerce is a sub-set of Knowledge Management because in e-commerce knowledge and information about products are taken and – through an IT-mediated interface – communicated to the customer in a mean-ingful fashion.

Thus the theories pertaining to e-commerce and the tools used (web 2.0 etc.) may be relevant to knowledge and information retrieval generally. Similarly pedagogy (learning and education) is included – again as a sub-set of Knowledge Management – because information has to be retrieved from an Information System in a human learnable form.

This new juxtaposition is needed because, on one hand as Kotler and Trias de Bes (2003) state; 'Companies need to innovate if they are to grow and prosper', but on the other hand 'an operational framework that distinguishes growth from non-growth small businesses does not exist' (Holmes & Zimmer, 1994). Thus this work and the resulting theory concentrates specifically on organizations the size of SMEs (after all, there are approximately 3.5 million SMEs in the UK, as opposed to a mere 7000 large companies) and focuses on revealing knowledge management-related and innovation-related growth factors for SMEs, especially those possess-ing no or little formally protected intellectual property. To put it bluntly, one often hears of 'innovative companies', but how do they become innovative? This work aims to illustrate factors theoretically important in producing innovations.

---

[1] Readers interested in e-commerce and outward-facing business models (which are not considered here) are referred to standard textbooks on the subject e.g. Turban and Volonino (2010).

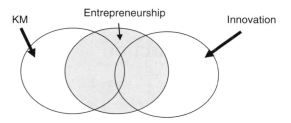

Figure 1.1 **Overlapping fields. Knowledge Management (left) may overlap with Innovation (right). However Entrepreneurship overlaps with both fields and forms a strong link between them. This is because Knowledge Management (at least in SMEs) is directed towards entrepreneurial aims on one hand and, on the other hand, Innovation is the tool for entrepreneurship[2].**

Innovations restructure value chains into more efficient and profitable forms – the basis of entrepreneurship. These innovations could be administrative (e.g. in restructuring, in marketing, etc.) or technical. The jumping off point could easily be Tidd et al. (2001, p.45) who state 'Success in innovation appears to depend on two key ingredients – technical resources (people, equipment, knowledge, money etc.) and the capabilities in the organization to manage them'. Unfortunately Tidd et al. (2001) do not follow up on this theme and indeed Atherton and Hannon (2001) again remark that there has been 'a paucity of research' on how innovation can arise and spread in small companies. This gap is addressed here using a basic mathematical model. The point of this modelling is to illuminate how to cultivate processes of knowledge use and as such, should not be confused with pursuing knowledge per se; the model presented defines the extremes of the innovation landscape and some of the common individual trails, paths or streams – knowledge management techniques and systems – which decorate that landscape. As such, the model is like a map, insomuch as it shows the peaks that can be attained and some short cuts to get there, but companies, buffeted by the katabatic winds of the Porterian Forces (Porter, 1980) acting upon them, will have to work out their own best route themselves: The model presented here is convincing, semi-quantitative and powerful, but it is not a fix-all recipe for guaranteed success, at the end of the day a map is just a map, not a perfect representation of reality and is certainly not guaranteed to prevent you from falling down pot holes!

---

[2] Entrepreneurship is defined as an academic discipline in management and economics. In the framework of economics, entrepreneurship is an exception to classical input–output economics. In a social and management framework the entrepreneur is often an active 'change agent', using 'creative destruction' and disintermediation: The entrepreneur consciously uses innovation and creativity as tools to achieve enterprise. In the model presented here, by extension, Knowledge Management promotes innovation to drive the enterprise in an entrepreneurial direction. Note that 'Entrepreneurial' means establishing new value chains and may thus not equate to cash profit, as thus is equally applicable to charities and other non-profit/not for profit organizations, including Public Sector ones.

GENERAL INTRODUCTION · INTRODUCTION TO KNOWLEDGE MANAGEMENT · INTRODUCTION TO INNOVATION · INTRODUCTION TO ENTREPRENEURSHIP · INTRODUCTION TO SMES · CONSTRUCTING KNOWLEDGE VALLEY · MANAGING FORMAL KNOWLEDGE · USING KVT TO IDENTIFY INNOVATION

2   1

GENERAL INTRODUCTION • INTRODUCTION TO KNOWLEDGE MANAGEMENT •
O INNOVATION • INTRODUCTION TO ENTREPRENEURSHIP • INTRODUCTION
RUCTING KNOWLEDGE VALLEY • MANAGING FORMAL KNOWLEDGE • USING
KVT TO IDENTIFY INNOVATION BOOSTING FACTORS • FACTORS THAT STOP INNOVATION
• A SUMMARY OF LESSONS LEARNT FROM KVT • RECOMBINING KNOWLEDGE AND
LEARNING PROVOKES INSPIRATION • SOME CONCLUSIONS AND SUMMING UP • CHOOSING
POSSIBLE TECHNOLOGIES • CALCULATE YOUR BENEFIT • LARGER ORGANIZATIONS

Part I **background**

Context and aims

In this part we are going to gain familiarity with the overarching thoughts behind Knowledge Management, Innovation and Entrepreneurship, with its product, SMEs. This section may be skimmed by advanced Business School students, although it is recommended for other students, including those of Information Systems.

At the end of this chapter the reader should be able to competently account for the major theories in the areas of Knowledge Management, Innovation, Entrepreneurship and have a reasonable understanding of new venture formation leading to the classification of SMEs.

GENERAL INTRODUCTION • INTRODUCTION TO KNOWLEDGE MANAGEMENT •
CTION TO INNOVATION • INTRODUCTION TO ENTREPRENEURSHIP • INTRODUCTION
• CONSTRUCTING KNOWLEDGE VALLEY • MANAGING FORMAL KNOWLEDGE • USING
KVT TO IDENTIFY INNOVATION BOOSTING FACTORS • FACTORS THAT STOP INNOVATION
• A SUMMARY OF LESSONS LEARNT FROM KVT • RECOMBINING KNOWLEDGE AND
LEARNING PROVOKES INSPIRATION • SOME CONCLUSIONS AND SUMMING UP • CHOOSING
POSSIBLE TECHNOLOGIES • CALCULATE YOUR BENEFIT • LARGER ORGANIZATIONS

2 introduction to knowledge management

Obviously knowledge has value – often high value; buying a house or investing in stocks and shares are two examples of areas where a knowledge shortfall can easily and rapidly lead to negative financial consequences. The importance of knowledge is steadily rising; there is a lot more knowledge in 1 Kg of post-industrial mobile phone or automotive vehicle than in 1 Kg of flour or similar agricultural product and consequently a Blackberry or Mercedes has a considerably higher kilo price than e.g. flour. Historically, the concept that knowledge has value stems from observations made during the Second World War, where it was found that workers building a second airplane took considerably less time that they took building the first. Arrow (1962) deduced that economically valuable knowledge was being gained by the process he called 'Learning by Doing'. Later, Bell (1973) postulated that knowledge ('intellectual assets') would form the basis of post-industrial society, a point taken up later by Peter Drucker '... The basic economic resource – "the means of production", to use the economist's term – is no longer capital, nor natural resources, nor "labour." It is will be knowledge ...' (Drucker, 1993). Since these early beginnings, a multitude of authors (e.g. Birkinshaw & Sheehan, 2002; Tidd et al. 2001) have tried to elaborate on how knowledge – like other corporate assets – could and should be managed. There appears to be a strong link between Knowledge Management and financial returns: Farrell (2000) polled 2000 organizations within Australia and found that a market orientation is positively related to a learning orientation within the company and that a learning orientation has a stronger significant positive effect on business performance than does market orientation. Simple data (like the postal codes of customers) can be drawn out of corporate databases by data mining and used in relatively straightforward exercises in e.g. targeted advertising. But unfortunately simple corporate data, while undoubtedly very close to market and useful on the small scale, is not where the competitive advantage of an organization is to be found. A 'fast economy' of rapid change requires flexible adaptive structures in an organization that can rapidly reorganize and self-organize in response to external stimuli. An organization's ability to do this is believed to reside in complex and context-sensitive knowledge which is difficult to codify because it exists in the heads of various individuals and is expressed when individuals interact. Thus Information Systems supports the necessary organizational adaptation by supporting and amplifying human potential. Information Systems organize information flow such that the required information or knowledge is correctly delivered in an understandable and learnable context relatively quickly. This is in contrast to Information Science (formerly known as Librarianship) which archives and retrieves information. The most wide-reaching method of archiving subject matter was invented in 1876 by the American librarian, Melvil Dewey (1851–1931).

2.1 Individual knowledge

One of the important early milestone works in the Knowledge Management field is Nonaka and Takeuchi's (1995) theory, which consists of two interacting knowledge spirals; the first is based on the distinction between tacit and explicit knowledge, the second on the distinction between the individual and the organization. To understand this, one must understand the difference between data, information and knowledge. Generally speaking, data is transformed into information after it has been contextualized, categorized, condensed and abstractified (i.e. raised to an abstract level). This is largely external to the individual and may, for example, be in a library. External knowledge is explicit knowledge that may have stemmed from an individual (e.g. the author of a book) but upon externalization it becomes fossilized, perhaps unreachable, perhaps meaningless to someone else (perhaps even meaningless to the author after some time!). But books do not walk around and do things, only humans do, so knowledge, to be useful, must be internalized: Nonaka and Takeuchi (1995, p.61) explain that '... human knowledge is created and expanded through social interaction between tacit knowledge and explicit knowledge ...'. Knowledge only becomes tacit knowledge after internalization; a process requiring comparison, connections and conversation. Above all, knowledge acquisition involves communication and learning. Thus possessing tacit knowledge gives an individual experience, contextual information and insight (e.g. in the above-mentioned examples concerning stock trading or real estate) and consequently enables that individual to construct a mental framework for evaluating and incorporating new experiences and information. Nonaka and Takeuchi (1995, p.57) explain that '... the engine of the entire knowledge-creation process...' is the so-called SECI cycle (Figure 2.1):

- Socialization (tacit to tacit)
- Externalization (from tacit to explicit)
- Combination (explicit to explicit)
- Internalization (explicit to tacit)

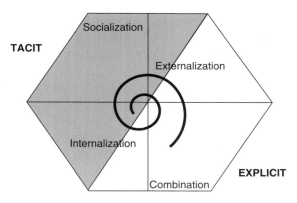

Figure 2.1 **The Nonaka and Takeuchi 'SECI-cycle' showing knowledge taking a diffuse spiral path from conception (an internal process within an individual) through sharing (socialization), making external (e.g. disseminating) and through several iterations hopefully arriving at an explicit combination which can be of practical use. Notice that knowledge alternates between being explicit and tacit on its travel around the spiral. Modified from Nonaka and Takeuchi (1995).**

Discussion about the exact nature of Nonaka and Takeuchi model still continues (e.g. Gourlay, 2006) as indeed do further models deriving from the Nonaka and Takeuchi model; the two major variants are those of Spender (1998) and Blackler (1995). Spender's notion highlights collective knowledge situated within an organization and underlines the important point that synergistic innovation should contribute to core competencies (since not contributing to core competencies will presumably waste effort and weaken the organization, see e.g. Quinn & Hilmer, 1995). Blackler identified five types of nicely alliterative knowledge – embrained, embodied, encultured, embedded and encoded – in an organization and points out that each of these can be on a gradient ranging from individual to collective. Blacklers view helps us appreciate that the way in which knowledge in an organization is managed will be a reflection of the dominant type already existing within that organization. For example, there will be differences in knowledge acquisition models between a biotech start-up and a new used-car dealership.

One of the main proponents of holistic management of knowledge assets is Max Boisot. Boisot (1998) adds a further dimension to the Nonaka and Takeuchi (1995) internalization phase: the SECI cycle is 2D, but by adding a third dimension (the third dimension is raising the data gathered to an abstract level), Boisot convincingly points out that 'truths' and insight gained in one area can be applied elsewhere. This is similar to a scientist performing experiments on grass or lettuce, the actual techniques used may not be applicable to other plants but in writing his thesis or publication the results are 'abstractified' into general concepts and theories which are then applicable to e.g. wheat, potatoes or beans – perhaps even to humans (or rabbits, or fish etc.) too.

For Boisot, knowledge follows a 3D closed path called the 'Social Learning Cycle' (SLC) in the 'I-Space' (information space). The I-Space can be visualized as the space enclosed by three axes (the X, the Y and the Z-axis) and where these different axes represent the degree to which knowledge is either tacit or codified, concrete or abstract and diffused or un-diffused. The six phases of the SLC are (Figure 2.2):

1. scanning (gathering observations)
2. problem-solving (mulling it over)
3. abstraction (is there a unifying principle or theory which makes the solution generic?)
4. diffusion (e.g. publication)
5. absorption (learning)
6. impacting (a change in behaviour)

It is important to realize that each stage follows logically and inevitably from its predecessor, and that the character of the knowledge evolves as it passes around the SLC. Thus, as tacit knowledge becomes more applied (perhaps with an externalization phase, i.e. Phases 4 and 5) and moves to Phase 6, it starts to express itself as experience, judgment and 'rule of thumb'. An example of this could be that experience of epidemics led to the classification of diseases ('pox', 'plague', etc.); scientists like Pasteur and Salmon peered down microscopes and published papers postulating that bacteria are the causative agents. Subsequently many books on microbiology were published that found a wider audience and were read by e.g. doctors and town planners, who taught the rules of hygiene and learnt to build sewers and provide clean water supplies, whereupon the knowledge continued along the SLC and finally became internalized – the rule of thumb that every child is taught – 'wash your hands!'

However, although each stage follows logically and inevitably from its predecessor, in the SLC, the velocity is not constant, as Von Hippel (1994) and Nonaka and Takeuchi (1995) point out, tacit knowledge is 'stickier' and slower to move.

I have always considered it somewhat unfair that the bacteria responsible for horrible illnesses are named after such famous scientists e.g. the enterobacter Salmonella (typhoid and several types of food poisoning) after the American epidemiologist Salmon and the Pasteurella (bubonic plague) after the French microbiologist Pasteur (actually better known for his research on Rabies). Surely this motivates scientists to remain obscure! Perhaps the commission that names such microorganisms should insist on anonymity.

GENERAL INTRODUCTION • **INTRODUCTION TO KNOWLEDGE MANAGEMENT** • INTRODUCTION TO INNOVATION • INTRODUCTION TO ENTREPRENEURSHIP • INTRODUCTION TO SMES • CONSTRUCTING KNOWLEDGE VALLEY • MANAGING FORMAL KNOWLEDGE • USING KVT TO IDENTIFY INNOVATION

8   2

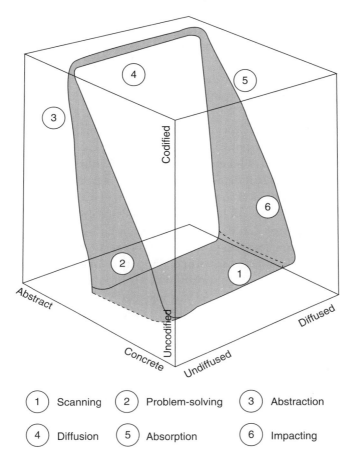

| 1 | Scanning | 2 | Problem-solving | 3 | Abstraction |
| 4 | Diffusion | 5 | Absorption | 6 | Impacting |

Figure 2.2 **The six phases of the SLC in I-space, taken from Boisot (1998) as modified by Mellor (2008). Reprinted with permission of the Oxford University Press.**

2.2 Organizational knowledge

Edith Penrose is usually credited with identifying knowledge as a key factor in the success of organizations. She set this out in her 1959 book *The Theory and Growth of the Firm* (Penrose, 1995). The previous neoclassical assumption had been that the things that cost money; labour, capital and resources (materials) were in short supply but that knowledge is free and instantly dispersible. It was true that knowledge is 'free' when it comes to e.g. the boiling point of a fluid or a coefficient of expansion of a metal etc., these can be looked up in widely available manuals. However by the

1960s organizations were working in specialized areas, so Penrose argued that the particular knowledge needed was actually hard to create and hard to learn (and therefore relatively expensive) while capital, labour and materials were actually generally available, although costing money. She also identified the organization itself as a source of embedded knowledge because while different individuals may grasp particular aspects, no individual can have complete knowledge of the entire operations of a successful growing organization after it has reached a certain size.

In contrast to individual knowledge, organizational knowledge (sometimes referred to as 'organizational memory') lies much more in the 'externalised' region as it will refer much less to the tacit knowledge of employees – e.g. knowledge about specific customers – and will much more often refer either to explicit knowledge like business rules or plain data-type information (e.g. databases of purchasers, and thus subject to analytical techniques like data warehousing and data mining). Unfortunately very little work has been done studying organizational knowledge in SMEs and as Sparrow (2001) and some other authors point out, the issues that face SMEs are not simple scaled-down replicas of those faced by large companies.

Teece (2000) has competently outlined the paths and processes larger corporations should take as parts of an institutionalized innovation strategy. In keeping with this 'big players' approach, the vast majority of studies on innovation and knowledge management have concentrated on major corporations (e.g. Baden-Fuller & Pitt, 1996; Etllie, 2000) and how they turn e.g. the ideas and knowledge-related products coming out of their large R&D departments into value. However a glance at the Yellow Pages will reveal that the vast majority of SMEs (used car dealerships, etc.) generally possess no R&D or formalized intellectual property like patents. As Sparrow (2001) again points out, SME owners often procrastinate until overwhelmed by fear of a specific and pressing business situation before they address knowledge issues (and indeed most other issues).

An additional criticism could be provoked by authors focusing on knowledge management between knowledge workers in e.g. the R&D department, to the exclusion of others: However the Barden Corporation (quoted in Chaston, 2000, p.133) receives over 50% of its suggestions for improvement from the factory floor workers, with only the minority from its graduate staff and this is certainly not an isolated case. Indeed one of the most-cited (and indeed classic) texts on knowledge management is Davenport and Prusak (1998), who begin their book promisingly with the message '... The only sustainable advantage a firm has comes from what it collectively knows, how efficiently it uses what it knows, and how readily it acquires and uses new knowledge ...', but again they go on to concentrate on large firms, e.g. the book includes numerous examples of successful knowledge projects at companies such as British Petroleum, 3M, Mobil Oil and Hewlett-Packard. Results from using 'big' case studies from these and other authors include e.g. various methods to determine the success of innovative strategy and tactics, including 'Balanced Scorecard', 'Organizational Network Analysis' or 'Data Envelope

Analysis' etc., but again, these again are of little use to SMEs who will typically use cheaper, more simple and last-minute methods, ranging from 'Discount Cash Flow' to 'Seat of Pants Navigation'.

In their breakthrough book, Davenport and Prusak (1998) explore the basis of knowledge sharing, concluding that motivation comes from three sources, all of which are based on an underlying platform of trust. These are,

- altruism (sharing or teaching for the fun of it),
- reciprocity (gaining credit in the "favour bank") or
- repute (enhanced status from being known as knowledgeable).

As said before, the Davenport and Prusak (1998) work is based on the analysis of large corporations and so the question is, do the same factors work, and to anything like the same extent, in SMEs? We decided to do some primary research and our analyses were based on the adoption of IT innovation in European SMEs (Mellor, 2005a), telephone interviews with 230 SMEs in the aerospace industry (McLean & Mellor, 2006) and 400 SMEs in various trades in South West London (Barnes et al. 2007). All these studies pointed to the trust factor being over-proportionally more important in small companies as opposed to large corporations. It may be that in small organizations, where all employees are (supposed to be) 'in the same boat' and 'pulling together', then trust is the important and all-pervasive social glue which is essential for SME function and progression. In clear contrast the situation of a high dependence on trust in SMEs, large corporations may depend much more on role descriptions and CV-banks, so whether a person is e.g. altruistic, becomes a relatively more prominent factor in large organizations.

Similarly the use of IT driven Information Systems[1] for Knowledge Management purposes is favoured in large corporations where work can be fractionated, complex and anonymous (the 'small cog in a large wheel' syndrome) plus that the often considerable IT development costs can be offset. But the use of IT systems for knowledge management is much less in SMEs, where the peer-to-peer 'social Ethernet' is predominant and considerably cheaper, e.g. having a shared directory of browser bookmarks or a shared server drive for documents. In these situations

---

[1] Information Systems supports the business processes of an organization by implementing a system of persons, data records and activities that process and share the data, ideas, knowledge and information in an organization, including both manual as well as automated processes. Lee (2001) states that '... research in the information systems field examines more than the technological system, or just the social system, or even the two side by side; in addition, it investigates the phenomena that emerge when the two interact.

However practical applications do often overlap with Information Technology, which the Information Technology Association of America (ITAA) defines as 'the study, design, development, implementation, support or management of computer-based information systems, particularly software applications and computer hardware'.

e.g. the imaginative use of email calendars is widespread, but it has a downside, e.g. the high degree of trust found in SMEs leaves them open to security issues.

2.3   Knowledge production and Capitalism

It is important to realize that as Capitalism evolves, so does knowledge production. Before the industrial revolution, craftsmen were often organized into Guilds (the 'Zunft') that functioned as protected pools of knowledge, because knowledge of how to make e.g. wooden barrels or other goods and so on had a cash value that was immediate, considerable and measurable. Some, like e.g. the Freemasons, would go to considerable lengths to protect 'their' proprietary 'secrets', often involving tedious rituals meant to impress the novice. Peter Drucker and others argued through the late 1960s and 1970s that pre-industrialization knowledge applied to processes and products and that during industrialization, knowledge was being re-focussed to human work, i.e. it was Fordist and task-machine based (see Chapter 1 for examples). There is a clear difference between someone with a long (pre-industrial) craft apprenticeship then, and the more simple training of any fairly randomly chosen individual (even today) in how to complete a well-defined task using an industrial machine, e.g. on a car assembly line. Post-war capitalism then saw the rise of knowledge workers as a class; large corporations had large R&D departments where these 'recognized' researcher elite existed in a quasi-apartheid situation with e.g. lowly production workers (which incidentally led to only such companies being included in studies of knowledge management!). At that time it was assumed that there only are a certain number of industries and that therefore understanding and controlling these will lead to optimal performance. Similarly with respect to knowledge, the view was that knowledge fitted into fairly stringently defined disciplines and any problems could be defined by academics or other professionals.

The IT revolution starting in the 1970s focussed attention on the possibilities of opening up new business areas; it showed that – against existing dogma – it was possible to make new business where no previous industry or business existed. These are the so-called 'sunrise' industries (e.g. Microsoft). Thus it was realized as the post-industrial 'Information Age' was ushered in, that fundamental knowledge could be produced in the context of application, thus discarding the traditional divisions between academic disciplines (much to the confusion of the University sector) and the concept of trans-disciplinarity was introduced.

Following this, the demise of the large corporation in the 1980s and 1990s and the simultaneous rise in the number of graduates, has created (or re-created) a situation where individuals, or small groups of individuals, 'possess' and protect scraps of knowledge that have market value. Examples of these could be para-medics, para-legal staff or indeed para-academic administration staff at universities! For

12   2

GENERAL INTRODUCTION · **INTRODUCTION TO KNOWLEDGE MANAGEMENT** · INTRODUCTION TO INNOVATION · INTRODUCTION TO ENTREPRENEURSHIP · INTRODUCTION TO SMES · CONSTRUCTING KNOWLEDGE VALLEY · MANAGING FORMAL KNOWLEDGE · USING KVT TO IDENTIFY INNOVATION want of a better term I call this 'rezunftification' and examples could be e.g. the conveyancing of real estate, where large fees are paid for a simple task because of the lack of clarity (bordering on deliberate mystification) about what it entails. Such individuals often cluster into ever-increasing numbers of ever-smaller 'professional bodies' or 'professional institutes', similar to the Zunft or Guild. Indeed, traditionally doctors, lawyers and so on have not, in the literature, been regarded as knowledge workers. However, when considering knowledge in the light of innovation and entrepreneurship (see section 2.1) then I believe that one could in fact make a case that they too can now be included because e.g. lawyers introduce new technology and business models, doctors open specialized private or 'poly' clinics and so on. As such, the market conditions for immaterial goods (i.e. knowledge) appears to be following a hyper-fragmentation path, exactly as described for markets for material goods (Kotler & Trias de Bes, 2003). Such knowledge can most often (sometimes only) become 'available' by incorporating relevant individuals

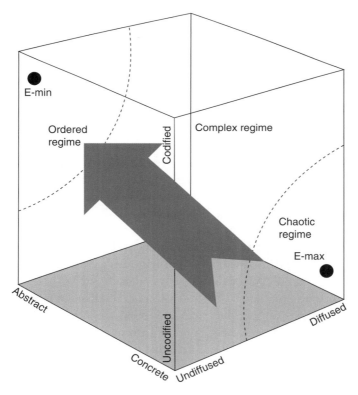

Figure 2.3 **Entropy (E) in the information space. Information Systems (the arrow) exist to lower the knowledge entropy and thus increase the value of knowledge in an organization or knowledge system. Modified from Boisot (1998) and reprinted with permission of the Oxford University Press.**

into a customer organization either on a consulting or other paid basis. But this is a dangerous path because non-available knowledge is, ultimately, a downwards trajectory to a subsistence existence.

2.4 Knowledge management techniques

Knowledge Management techniques (sometimes called knowledge management systems) are those which take knowledge from the state of being available (somehow, somewhere), to actually being used, presumably in a business or enterprise direction. The theoretical background is provided by Boisot (1998), whose theory of knowledge assets includes the recognition that different regions of the I-Space exist in different states of entropy (Figure 2.3).

In the vast majority of branches of science (e.g. the second law of thermodynamics), entropy is a measure of the disorder of a system. The concept of entropy is particularly notable because it is applied across several disciplines, e.g. physics, information theory and mathematics, and in particular in the second law of thermodynamics (where it is symbolized as S). Essentially, this is a quantification of information, so the amount of information in e.g. a computer file is equivalent to the $\log^2$ of the number of bits. However in information theory, entropy – sometimes known as self-information – is a measure of the uncertainty associated with a random variable (usually referring to the Shannon entropy) which quantifies – in the sense of an expected value – the mathematical (i.e. bits and bytes) amount of information contained in a message. The concept was introduced by Claude Shannon in 1948 and is expanded upon in the classic Shannon and Weaver book (1963) entitled *The Mathematical Theory of Communication*.

But let us get back to entropy: Entropy is at a minimum in ordered systems, i.e. that part of the I-Space where knowledge is not diffuse, is well codified and abstract. Where entropy is high then value is low: e.g. bound literature (like this book) is 'well ordered' and thus has low entropy and high value, but the individual pages, torn out and 'diffused' randomly (thrown) around the room, will have higher entropy and thus correspondingly less value.

A high entropy situation is the situation most often encountered in organizations; the workers apparently scattered around the organization each have scraps of useful information. The science of Information Systems generally, and knowledge management solutions (especially IT-driven knowledge management solutions) in particular, exist to bring order to the system, lowering the entropy and thus increasing the value. However techniques for sharing knowledge (e.g. across an organization, perhaps even a multi-national organization) demand that knowledge is externalized, but unfortunately knowledge externalization, in rapid learning regimes, rapidly becomes obsolete (Boisot, 1998). Everyone who has had even a minimal website (not to mention a large corporate intranet) knows that it is not constructing a website, but rather updating it, that is the major challenge – so please construct data structures that obviate the need to have to update the databases and tables in several places! Moreover, Boisots' theory states that short-cuts across the SLC are not allowed and therefore that efforts should concentrate on increasing the speed of throughput, i.e. using automation to shorten the time taken to get from Phase 1 to Phase 6 without missing out the intervening stages.

Often computer-aided learning (or 'e-learning', see e.g. Mellor & Mellor, 2004 or Dreyfus, 2001, for details and discussion) is used under the assumption that it can accelerate the throughput time. Simple examples of e-learning include e.g. the 'help' files or the 'office assistants' built into many common office software packages.

Case 1

e-learning is a subset of Knowledge Management

E-learning: an example showing that the benefits may not be where you expect them (a case study first published partly in Mellor & Mellor, 2004 and again in Mellor, 2008).

Students on a conversion Masters course and learning programming at the IT University of Copenhagen took part in a series of experiments to see if e-learning could help them learn. All of the students attended regular classes but half of the students were given an e-learning version of the course material as well. Quizzes were built into the e-learning material at the beginning, mid-way and end points of the courses to check that participants had progressed in their learning. But when the overall exam results were published the group that had used the e-learning material had a lower average grade than the control group!

Further investigations showed that, in the control group, good learners learnt well but the poor learners became de-motivated and left the course. Conversely, in the group exposed to the e-learning material, there was a much lower dropout rate among poor performers and it was their (still poor) exam performance that lowered the group average.

Thus, although e-learning did help improve the performance of poor perform-ers, the main effect of digitalizing the material and producing interactive e-learning material was to encourage poor learners and thus reduce costly drop-out rates.

Students who got low marks (those falling below the range of the control group)	Students who got high marks (those falling within the range of the control group)
Characterized by a 'soft' first degree background: social science, language, etc.	Characterised by a 'hard' first degree background: physics etc.
Thought the e-learning material was: • easy to use • helpful • thought they had learnt something Did progress from low to higher as measured by Quiz results	Thought the e-learning material was: • childishly easy • not worth doing • learnt nothing new Always scored high in Quizzes

The lessons learnt were:

- Those already at 'proficient' level were not able to progress to 'expert' level with the material provided, because this material was pitched to a broad band from 'advanced beginner' to 'proficient' levels (referring to the Dreyfus Model of Skills Acquisition, see Dreyfus & Dreyfus, 1986).
- In a class of mixed levels of expertise, e-learning material may lower the average final performance, but this is irrelevant because those who would have scored high will score high anyway, those who would have scored low will perform better, but the major advantage is that retention rates among 'poor' performers are increased.
- Those with a 'soft' background were capable of completing these rather technical courses, but they will tend to drop-out unless their interest is engaged by a different type of delivery in parallel e.g. the e-learning material.
- Thus e-learning 'plug-ins' should deliberately be pitched low, aiming at the lowest common denominator, with the explicit aim of increasing retention in this segment, rather than improving the performance of the already good participants.
- This is particularly important when prototyping, don't get a super-user to test the beta, get test subjects from the lower end of the spectrum, otherwise your results will be skewed in a negative direction.

Thus e-learning,[2] seen through the lens of Information Systems, becomes a subset of Knowledge Management (although note that although e-learning overlaps with Business Information Systems, it is not a complete subset of Business Information Systems). Against this background Cole-Gomolski (1997) asserted 'the idea behind knowledge management is to stockpile knowledge and make it accessible to others via a searchable application', however Lagerström and Andersson (2003), report that the most powerful influence on knowledge spread in organizations is social, and that e.g. IT systems made little significant impact. Similarly Huysman and de Wit (2004) using survey data, as well as Gelepithis (2005), who reviewed the artificial intelligence (AI) approach, all noted the very limited success of conventional IT-based knowledge management techniques, and then only for large firms which (a) can afford the overheads and (b) which tend to move relatively slowly when compared to the (theoretically) more nimble SMEs.

A further barrier is that in organizations, individuals are unwilling to externalize their knowledge (i.e. complete the essential step from tacit to explicit knowledge) – also because they may be poached by competitors: For example, in 1997 I thought it would be a good idea to put the names of our experts on the website;

---

[2] e-learning is meant here in an adult education context because first children do not learn by instruction but rather by imitation and secondly there are (hopefully) few children employed in SMEs or other commercial enterprises (the subject of this book)!

but my idea was shot down by more experienced people because (and this was true, I was wrong) that this would simply lead to headhunting from competitors: Transparency is not always good. A summary of common barriers to establishing a common knowledge base include:

- **Usage:** it is easier for an individual to ask a co-worker rather than look it up. This is especially prevalent in IT-related tasks.[3]
- **Content**: employees are unable or reluctant to input their knowledge, reasoning that doing so will decrease their personal value.
- **Technical:** recalling the stored content in a meaningful context.
- **Spiralling costs:** pedagogy and programming rarely work well together, leading to expensive delays.

Indeed, IT-driven knowledge management systems will often not normally progress beyond an intranet-like stage and may be questionable value for money (a '... misguided capital investment...' see Thompson & Walsham, 2004) although some authors (e.g. Liebowitz, 2002) wax lyrical about certain specialist software applications. The popularity of IT systems could be based upon the fact that they are easier for managers to grasp than reorganizing corporate structure to facilitate communicative interactions (Thompson & Walsham, 2004). Several authors (e.g. Wilson, 2002) regard such systems not as being systems for knowledge management, but rather repackaged forms of information management. Marr and Spender (2004) sum up the situation by concluding '... the time has come to move on from ... simplistic data or information assets towards the more dynamic ... complex role of knowledge in the value creation process ...' Indeed, the trend appears to be dropping the more static proprietary document management systems like MS-Sharepoint in favour of e.g. Xoops, Joomla or Drupal. Furthermore, the effect of systems like Moodle or the similar Mahara and virtual reality environments like SimCity (probably as Open Sim), Second Life or Wonder World on learning is as yet unknown, as are the enabling effects of technical advances such as Web2.0, SOA and Mashups (see Segaran, 2007; Yee, 2008) and may well be over-hyped, as in the case of Wikis (Tapscott & Williams, 2008), which rarely last for periods longer that one year. In particular, the suitability of XML in conjunction with data warehousing means that it is eminently suitable for mining into 'the long tail' of accumulated but seldom-used information (Anderson, 2007), but unfortunately XML is sadly underused, or at least underused in its 'pure' form.

---

[3] In an organization of 2500 people that was having trouble with Office programmes like Word; thus a link was established on all workers PC Desktop to the ECDL material and help files (that explain how to use Word and other Office programmes). Four years later (i.e. 10,000 man years later) it was found that no-one at all had used the material!

In section 2.2 we discussed the value of trust as an essential pre-requisite for knowledge sharing. This can, of course, be reinforced by organization-wide incentives and rewards that are quite independent of Information Systems:

Case 2

Simple HR methods can promote knowledge sharing

In an SME of 120 employees, selling products in the travel services area, I put a new reward structure in place: Previous to 1998, salary levels were wildly different between employees and depended on the individuals' ability to argue their case in one-off annual meetings with their line manager. This was replaced with a transparent system where employees were all rewarded almost equally, with only a slight rise in salary for length of service (which was presumed to reflect knowledge/experience level), but on top of this came a substantial variable bonus, which was awarded according to three criteria:

1. individual selling performance (i.e. reward for actual input)
2. group selling performance (to stop sellers 'poaching' customers from their colleagues)
3. company-wide bonus (based on the company end-of-year overall performance)

Upon review two years later it was found that the second bonus contribution in particular had acted as an enormous incentive for individuals to actively share their knowledge – and innovations in best practice – with their peers: e.g. instead of hoarding information, and perhaps thereby risking losing a client, employees started leaving exhaustive notes with their colleagues on exactly what to do if that client phoned, etc.

Such measures align teamwork and business goals with individual targets and are reflected in a preliminary model for knowledge management in SMEs, presented below. In this model a signal of some kind triggers a cycle resulting in some kind of content being accessed. How this is done may well be social, and the result is an interaction of some kind (e.g. an informed process set in motion or completed, etc.).

The above model (Figure 2.4) may be especially relevant to knowledge-based SMEs like those in highly specialized services with high margins, or e.g. small software houses, although manufacturing SMEs e.g. specialist engineering providers, could also benefit from it. Perceptive readers will realize that Figure 2.4 is an interpersonal/organizational (i.e. Information Systems) perspective of Figure 2.1, the Nonaka and Takeuchi 'SECI-cycle' and the stages of this model and the SECI model are compared with the ICDT model (derived from e-commerce) in Table 12.3.

GENERAL INTRODUCTION · **INTRODUCTION TO KNOWLEDGE MANAGEMENT** · INTRODUCTION TO INNOVATION · INTRODUCTION TO ENTREPRENEURSHIP · INTRODUCTION TO SMES · CONSTRUCTING KNOWLEDGE VALLEY · MANAGING FORMAL KNOWLEDGE · USING KVT TO IDENTIFY INNOVATION

18   2

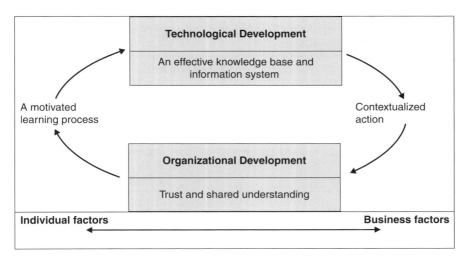

Figure 2.4 **A model for knowledge management in SMEs: trust and shared under-standing should provide the motivation for learning in individuals which again contributes to managing a usable knowledge base in a technical system. Using this effectively should result in the proper actions being taken in the correct business context.**

2.5 Organizational learning

We have seen that knowledge may be more tacit, or more explicit, at the level of the individual. For knowledge to spread and innovation to occur some learning must take place in groups and models of the spread of innovation as a group process will be addressed in Chapter 3, section 3.4. Individuals and groups can learn something new and adapt their behaviour accordingly. Organizational learning is where the learning occurring in individuals and groups impact the behaviour of the organization. Normally we say that this is not just using innovations to improve e.g. production processes, but it has a significant impact on the organizations strategic business model. Clearly this is relatively rare, as organizations may be operating in environments with strict business imperatives. Nonetheless it is worth considering how the emerging mass of new and recombined knowledge may communicate with the organization's leaders (i.e. the layer determining the business model) in order to raise awareness at senior management level.

The multidisciplinary nature of managing knowledge into organizational learning is expressed in Table 2.1:

In Chapters 3 and 6 (especially Chapter 6, section 6.1.2) arguments are presented that in small organizations it is recombining the diversity of knowledge and experience within the workforce which makes SMEs (see Chapter 5)

Table 2.1 **Illustrating the multidiscipline aspects of Knowledge Management and learning in organizations.**

Task	Major discipline
Mixing and recombining workforce knowledge	Socialization processes
Enabling knowledge flow and giving structure	Leadership and management processes
Facilitating and supporting knowledge processes	Information Systems
Operational communication	Information Technology and e-Learning

nimble and the major barrier in growing organizations is the growing transaction costs for this communication. As illustrated in table 2.1, this recombination of often tacit knowledge is a socialization process, the results of which are given shape and form – hopefully in an entrepreneurial direction – by the leadership layer. While strategies can be simple (e.g. rotating shift workers so everyone meets everyone else, or bonus schemes as mentioned in section 2.4), clearly this rests on having correctly configured Information Systems (IS), the operational manifestation of which is the hardware and software of the IT department. However as organizational learning involves learning, there is also a pedagogical aspect to this – and as shown in section 2.4. Computer-delivered pedagogy is basically e-Learning and we will return to this theme in Chapter 11, section 11.4.

The interplay between these various disciplines can be represented as in Figure 2.5.

As can be seen, the various disciplines have to work closely together, and difficulties in coordinating the mindsets of the various actors involved will increase the transaction costs for such projects. In the above figure (Figure 2.5) a second input into the workforce knowledge is considered new knowledge. This can be that coming in from IT systems like a CRM or ERP system, or that represented by new employees, or may be from e.g. hired consultants. IT can help new employees by presenting them with business rules, flow-charts of procedures, organigrams and so on, but spreading the knowledge gained from e.g. consultants reports is quite difficult unless it is marked up with e.g. XML tags for various categories of reader, possibly identified through Active Directory (i.e. login name) or digital signatures, security tokens and so on.

Please note that Figure 2.5 in no way represents IT architecture, indeed each domain may well require different variations on Business Process Management (accounting, finance etc.) both horizontally as well as vertically (e.g. executive leaders will require more 'dashboard'-type elements). What Figure 2.5 represents

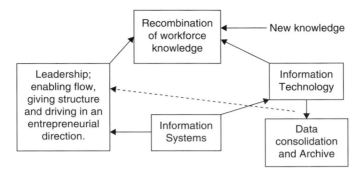

Figure 2.5 **The roles of socialization, leadership, Information Systems and Information Technology in organizational learning.**

Note: The dotted line (performance management) is included to underline the importance of providing key indicator reports and decision support gathered from the data archive by data mining (i.e. a feedback loop to monitor performance) although admittedly one could justifiably argue that this process proceeds through Information Systems and therefore does not need a separate arrow.

is as follows; business process excellence underlies the competitive performance of an organization and areas could be:

- better customer satisfaction
- cost reduction
- improved cycle/order fulfilment time
- improved quality
- higher productivity

So Figure 2.5 is not a magic bullet addressing how to succeed in these areas, rather a stepping off point as to how to use IT to help generate ideas as to how to succeed in these areas.

In considering the diverse nature of the IT one should not only consider the use of IT in operational support of the recombination (and adding) of knowledge, and its retrieval in context and according to pedagogical principles, but also other aspects (however security is not considered here, as the principles of Figures 2.4 and 2.5 are imagined to proceed on a trusted network behind effective firewalls). One large aspect is to accumulate data, but in such a way that it is still useful (there are many jokes about Knowledge Management (KM) meaning 'knowledge museum'!). This may be previous knowledge data or indeed hard data, like sales (products, customers etc.). In this context it should provide tools and services to leadership and other knowledge workers to mine these archives. However putting the results of data-mining to practical use is quite a different task, requiring decision-making software and concept management tools, aimed at senior management, who will often use the results of data-mining as a measure of performance.

Thus if performance indicators correlate to the emerging mass of new and recombined knowledge then the organizations leaders (i.e. the layer determining the business model) may become aware of this by using decision-making software and concept management tools like NVIVO, Microsoft Decision Explorer and Frontier Analyst (which are just a few from many).

The tasks of the IT used are thus very complex and varies with different target groups. This again underlines the importance of getting the right Information Systems (IS) structure in place early in the life of the organization and early mistakes can be deadly (see Table 12.1).

2.6 Similarities between knowledge management and innovation

There have been publications attempting to unify the two fields of knowledge management and innovation: Mascitelli (2000) states '...evolutionary product improvements often follow predictable trajectories, breakthrough innovations involve unexpected leaps of creativity and insight...' and 'breakthrough innovations result from the harnessing of tacit knowledge...' but again, as queried in section 2.1, such studies have concentrated on rather narrow areas, typically about sharing tacit knowledge in R&D departments in larger organizations. Although, on a general note, many of these observations may be applicable to SMEs because they rest to some extent on the nature of the individual, Carneiro (2000) agrees that '...knowledge development is a fruitful background where incremental innovation may be attempted...'

Benefiting from the incredible clarity of hindsight, one can see that the major weakness of the Nonaka and Takeuchi (1995) theory is that it does not include knowledge gathering by extensive external networks. The importance of networks for Innovation was recognized by Rothwell (1992) but this epiphany was not fed into Knowledge Management, but instead slowly into Entrepreneurship, so earlier works on Knowledge Management (e.g. Nonaka & Takeuchi, 1995) concentrate on knowledge sharing in large organizations and thus have not taken into account more recent developments in our understanding of this related discipline (indeed, Entrepreneurship was only accepted as an academic discipline in the UK in 2000). In contrast to classical Knowledge Management, Entrepreneurship theory (a decade later!) recognizes the supreme importance of networks (e.g. Bessant & Tidd, 2007; Mellor, 2003a, 2008). Relying originally on the works of e.g. Rothwell (1992), Entrepreneurship lays much weight on external networks to provide 'knowledge on demand' and 'just-in-time knowledge'. Thus Entrepreneurship provides the essential crossover link between Knowledge

Management and Innovation because on one hand the environmental context of Knowledge Management in those organizations implementing it, is entrepreneurial, and on the other hand Entrepreneurship depends heavily on Innovation (e.g. Drucker, 1985).

Put in a pseudo mathematical context, it can be seen from the previous sections that Knowledge Management involves a transmitter and a receiver. In its most simple form, this is a 1-to-1 relationship, e.g. an apprenticeship, on the socialization (tacit to tacit) level. This diffusion relationship can be described as:

$$1 \rightarrow 2$$

i.e. where previously 1 person had the knowledge, now 2 people have it. Obviously with an increasing degree of externalization – as well as the consequent dilution of impact – this can be scaled up to 1-to-many (e.g. classroom teaching) or many-to-many (e.g. blogging) relationships.

Innovation, in contrast, can be described differently:

$$1 + 1 = > 2$$

i.e. when 2 individuals meet their interaction – mutual inspiration, an unexpected conjunction of different perspectives – gives rise to a creative or innovative idea or concept which has not previously existed – the much misquoted 'synergy effect'. In this case the innovative niveau has been raised not to 2, but to 3 (or at least a figure larger than 2) because something exists now which had not previously existed. Furthermore the source knowledge can be either explicit or tacit, or both. As Diegel puts it, 'over an undefined period of time, something magically occurs and a good, workable idea is generated as an output' (Diegel, 2005). To understand this properly it is necessary to further explore what innovation is.

GENERAL INTRODUCTION • INTRODUCTION TO KNOWLEDGE MANAGEMENT •
CTION TO INNOVATION • INTRODUCTION TO ENTREPRENEURSHIP • INTRODUCTION
• CONSTRUCTING KNOWLEDGE VALLEY • MANAGING FORMAL KNOWLEDGE • USING
KVT TO IDENTIFY INNOVATION BOOSTING FACTORS • FACTORS THAT STOP INNOVATION
• A SUMMARY OF LESSONS LEARNT FROM KVT. • RECOMBINING KNOWLEDGE AND
LEARNING PROVOKES INSPIRATION. • SOME CONCLUSIONS AND SUMMING UP • CHOOSING
POSSIBLE TECHNOLOGIES • CALCULATE YOUR BENEFIT • LARGER ORGANIZATIONS

3   introduction to innovation

Often one hears the terms discovery, invention and innovation used as synonyms, however they are quite distinct. Discovery is a new addition to knowledge, often in the physical, biological or social sciences. Theoretical knowledge is obtained from observations and the experimental testing of hypotheses while practical knowledge is obtained from practice: e.g. the practical knowledge acquired by a workforce in making new machinery operate well. Invention can result in a new device or process whereas innovation is often a better way of doing things. An innovation improves performance in goal-directed behaviour, e.g. re-election politics or personal lifestyle, as measured by any applicable or relevant criterion (e.g. profit maximization). One simple example of this difference could be spreadsheet programs like Excel. The invention is the computer (hardware) and its various parts, including the software (e.g. Excel). However, using spreadsheets to plan hourly work in an office is an innovation. Invention is promoted by discovery (esp. in biology) whereas innovation is promoted by invention (esp. in industrial engineering and business). As science advances it creates opportunities for new inventions. However to develop economic value, massive knowledge is needed and indeed modern airplanes needed the development of the whole science of aerodynamics. To make a profit out of this (e.g. the commercial airline business), the innovation has to be applied to the market – often in the form of entrepreneurship. To continue the aerospace example, the entrepreneurial end could be Ryanair or Easyjet. Some authors e.g. Prescott and Van Slyke (1996) refer to such examples as 'Technology Cluster Innovation'. Clearly even this superficial overview as given in Table 3.1 illustrates the aerospace meta-cluster, which consisting of three overlapping clusters, ranging from mostly inventive, through mostly innovative, to mostly entrepreneurial (although organizations on the left side of the table, like Boeing, are also entrepreneurial).

Thus it can be seen that the vast majority of SMEs are simply entrepreneurial, being flexible or specialized enough to re-combine known inventions, processes or innovations for a new market, without themselves having registered a patent, or made a spectacular invention or any radical or revolutionary new innovation.

Table 3.1 **Division of the meta-cluster 'Aerospace' into three clusters according to the inventive character (e.g. based on patents) at the left, the mostly innovative in the centre and the more purely entrepreneurial applications on the right.**

Branch	Products	Application and exploitation
Aerodynamic and engineering research.	Many different types of aeroplanes, helicopters, rockets etc.	Many different airline companies with different target groups

Drucker (1985) says that all change is a source of innovative opportunity, including:

- the unexpected
- the incongruity
- process need
- changes in industry or market structure
- demographics
- changes in perception, mood, meaning
- new knowledge

Innovation and entrepreneurship are often associated with the terms 'value chain'[1] and 'creative destruction': entrepreneurship often uses change and innovation to modify the value chain, a process often accompanied by disintermediation and another, associated, phenomenon, 'creative destruction'. Typically with the introduction of new technology (e.g. the Internet) a new business situation is created and this destroys the old. Luckily for the small entrepreneur, existing large firms are seldom capable of making major shifts in technology. The management of existing firms has invested enormous amounts of man-years in understanding their particular business and perfecting lucrative 'cash cow' products while they have little expertise in the 'new(er) technology'. For example, why did railroad firms not open automobile factories? Probably their knowledge of the old prevented them from appreciating the new (or perhaps the emergent technologies were first in a humiliating infant state, leading them to be overlooked until too late, e.g. the first 'automobile' was a steam-driven prototype not able to exceed 3 mph, a then-laughable alternative to swift steam locomotives). Even though innovation is now more widely appreciated in management, the present-day example of the demise of the national post and telegraph companies, the public

---

[1] The expression 'value chain' is also used in an intra-organizational sense, referring to a bundle of factors, affecting value from when a product enters the firm, to when it leaves it. Obviously in such cases, in contrast to above, 'added value' is an important factor. Furthermore, several 'value chains' may make up a 'value system'. For a detailed discussion of this topic, see Porter (1990) and Chapter 4, section 4.2.

and private telephone companies struggling to master and dominate the mobile market, some by being Internet providers, others not, shows that the transition is not simple. This underlies the need for understanding how innovation spreads through organizations and cultures.

Large organizations have felt the need to 'formalize' the acquisition of innovation, and several theories exist addressing how to do this, e.g. Boisot (1998) and Stacey (1996). However, these theories are largely unknown among SMEs (see e.g. Barrow, 1998). Indeed the evolution of these two types of organization is quite different, including that large organizations often have the philosophy 'what must we do in order to be stronger and exist well into the future?' while small organizations operate under more Darwinian constraints; they try to survive tomorrow in the sure knowledge that if they do not, then they will quickly be replaced.

3.1 What is innovation?

In his review of the literature, Van Grundy (1987) made the distinction between innovation and creativity, and indeed several other researchers (e.g. Shepard, 1967; Thompson, 1965; Pierce & Dalbecq, 1977; Zaltman et al. 1973) define innovation as excluding creativity. Other examples include 'first or early use of an idea' (Becker & Whisler, 1967), 'the adoption of means or ends that are new' (Downs & Mohr, 1976), 'the adoption of change that is new' (Knight, 1967), 'an idea, practice or object that is perceived as new' (Rogers, 1983) and 'adopted changes considered new' (Daft & Becker, 1978). There may be many, who have difficulty with accepting change that is not new, or something new appearing with change having happened or ideas not being creative. Kanter (1983) states that 'innovation is the generation, acceptance and implementation of new ideas, processes, products and services' and adds that 'innovation involves creative use as well as original invention'. Thus it appears:

Invention + application = innovation
Creativity + application = innovation

So which is more important, invention innovation or creativity innovation (or a third factor)? Porter (1990, p.74) states that 'companies achieve competitive advantage through acts of innovation' and again later (Porter, 1998) that 'much innovation is mundane and incremental, depending more on an accumulation of small insights than on a single major technological breakthrough'. The finding that the sum of many incremental innovations can have a very large impact is also supported by other research (e.g. Bessant, 1999). This implies that invention actually plays a minor part in the process of value creation. Indeed Valery (1999)

26   3

GENERAL INTRODUCTION · INTRODUCTION TO KNOWLEDGE MANAGEMENT · **INTRODUCTION TO INNOVATION** · INTRODUCTION TO ENTREPRENEURSHIP · INTRODUCTION TO SMES · CONSTRUCTING KNOWLEDGE VALLEY · MANAGING FORMAL KNOWLEDGE · USING KVT TO IDENTIFY INNOVATION stated 'innovation has more to do with the pragmatic search for opportunity than with romantic ideas about serendipity or lonely pioneers pursuing their vision against all odds'.

Thus it would appear that to enhance innovation, one must simply apply creativity. This idea has been important in spreading the works of e.g. Edward DeBono. For example, DeBonos' book *Serious Creativity* (1996) begins with the words 'If I were to sit down and say to myself I need a new idea here ... I could quietly and systematically apply a deliberate technique of lateral thinking ... and in 10 to 20 seconds I should have some new ideas'. All humans think and are to some degree able to solve problems. Why then are not all humans creative (by self-definition)? To postulate that they have not read DeBono's books is not a satisfying answer. The worst complication is that creativity is neither precisely defined nor measurable. Parkhurst (1999, p.18) produced probably the best definition of creativity by stating that creativity is 'the ability or quality displayed when solving hitherto unsolved problems, when developing original and novel solutions to problems others have solved differently, or when developing original and novel (at least to the originator) products'. This definition is still imprecise, because, for example it lacks quantitative measures of how original a product (be it a poem, a painting or a patent) must be to qualify as the result of a creative process. Furthermore, it opens a significant overlap between creativity and 'mere' problem solving.

In sum, it appears that significant creativity belongs to a middle layer of innovation ('creativity innovation'), and that there exists a layer below, which depends on the simple diversity existing between humans ('diversity innovation') (Figure 3.1). To put it simply, talking to somebody with a different background may deliver the problem's solution right in your lap, without any significant degree of invention and/or creativity, i.e. a kind of mutual inspiration or synergy. This idea contradicts classical Taylorism (the view that workers have few skills and it is sufficient to give them specific tasks and orders) and is more in line with TQM (e.g. the Barden Corporation, quoted in Chaston, 2000, p.133 is only one example of many organizations receiving suggestions for improvement from the shop floor workers).

Thus it becomes more obvious that innovation – like invention – is time dependant (clearly in inventing the steam engine in 2010 and applying it to the cotton industry is not an innovation), however innovation – in contrast to invention – is also context dependant; Henry Ford copied production processes that he had seen at a Chicago meat plant (an abattoir owned by an acquaintance) and 'simply' applied them in the motor industry (Chaston, 2000), creating a car assembly line out of a cow disassembly line.

The traditional economic perspective of the Schumpeterian hypothesis (see Schumpeter, 1942) addresses the relationship between company size and the efficiency, or productivity, of the innovative process, especially as to whether there are

BOOSTING FACTORS • FACTORS THAT STOP INNOVATION • A SUMMARY OF LESSONS LEARNT FROM KVT • RECOMBINING KNOWLEDGE AND LEARNING PROVOKES INSPIRATION • SOME CONCLUSIONS AND SUMMING UP • CHOOSING POSSIBLE TECHNOLOGIES • CALCULATE YOUR BENEFIT • LARGER ORGANIZATIONS 3

27

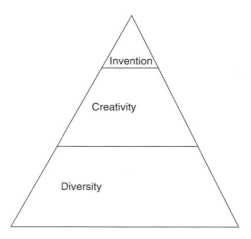

Figure 3.1 **Illustrating that innovation can come from three sources, the application of invention, the application of creativity and the application of diversity, where the 'mundane' diversity is responsible for the majority of everyday problem solving (incremental innovation) and invention is responsible for the few radical innovations.**

economies of scale in innovation. This hypothesis appears to hold true for large companies; for example; Palmer (2004) reports that L'Oreal have 28,000 patents, Proctor & Gamble have over 30,000 active patents and that IBM applies for typically more that 3000 patents each year. Clearly this is a pipeline production where a few patents more or less may not matter, so there appear to be economies of scale in invention, but equally clearly, this addresses only those innovations (technological and perhaps radical/vertical innovations) at the apex of the pyramid, because there cannot be economies of scale in e.g. diversity innovation (see Chapter 3, section 3.2). Indeed SMEs are known to be responsible for creating new knowledge (in the form of patents, etc.) to a lesser extent than large companies are (McAdam & Reid, 2001), yet they are relentlessly innovative ... or dead!

Later, in Chapter 6, section 6.1.2, we will see that it is these transaction costs associated with communication, which is the limiting factor for diversity (horizontal/incremental) innovation.

3.2 The concepts of invention-, creativity- and diversity-innovation

Invention innovation is defined here as the application of an invention or discovery. Invention innovation tends to be vertical and radical (see Figure 3.3). The vast majority of SMEs are not built around a new technological (and thus patented) breakthrough. However, a glimpse at the Yellow Pages will show that very

28 3

GENERAL INTRODUCTION · INTRODUCTION TO KNOWLEDGE MANAGEMENT · **INTRODUCTION TO INNOVATION** · INTRODUCTION TO ENTREPRENEURSHIP · INTRODUCTION TO SMES · CONSTRUCTING KNOWLEDGE VALLEY · MANAGING FORMAL KNOWLEDGE · USING KVT TO IDENTIFY INNOVATION many have some form of protection on either their image or products (registered trade marks etc.). Thus these forms of protection are secondary and merely serve to confound base imitators – therefore they are not considered further here.

Creativity: Here it is not the point to explain phenomena such as Shakespeare, Beethoven, Michelangelo or Aristotle. Creative innovation is used here in the sense of being the tool used to achieve differential advantage at the market place. Both Greiner (1972) and McDonald and Christopher (2003) say that the company begins with 'creativity'. Originally this meant in part the creation of a company (new venture formation is by definition creative, but is however probably in itself a mundane task). Here, in contrast, it is taken as being the central business idea. In the context of SMEs it may mean 'why not open a (theme) restaurant' where 'theme' is a word of your choice, 40 years ago in the UK it could have been 'pizza', now it could be e.g. 'Alaskan' offering e.g. fried huskies. For established companies it may be e.g. 'we build boats to keep water out, so why not build water tanks, to keep water in'. Certainly the individual entrepreneurs often mentioned in standard textbooks about entrepreneurship, e.g. the late Anita Roddick (Body Shop) and Richard Branson (Virgin), achieved fame and fortune not by applying new technological inventions, but by applying creative business models. The same goes for many large organizations, e.g. Marks & Spencer, Tesco and so on. Creativity innovation is not central to this work because the organizations we are dealing with, to wit SMEs, are considered to have already been established (i.e. the venture has been created).

Diversity innovation is most often a peer-to-peer phenomenon, i.e. horizontal and incremental innovation (see Figure 3.3). It can be best summed up as 'sometimes the answer just falls into your lap', or 'mutual inspiration' or 'synergy'. A typical environment could be simply an informal talk with someone from a different background.

Case 3

Mutual inspiration; radical and incremental

One historically important case was the clergyman Joseph Priestly, from a poor Yorkshire background, who met the wealthy Frenchman Antoine Lavoisier at dinner in 1774. Their mutual inspiration led to the discovery of oxygen and as such overturned the alchemical concept of Phlogiston, thereby creating the discipline of Chemistry.

Henry Ford drew his inspiration for the car assembly line from an acquaintance that had had an abattoir, where carcasses were circulated hung from a rail and each butcher performed one action, so the car assembly line sprang from a cow disassembly line!

Other cases can be much more mundane. A shoe manufacturer made expensive shoe soles using a plastic-injection moulding technique. A down-market retailer came along with a big order, the problem was that the existing moulds featured the expensive name brand 'built-in', and the outlay for new moulds would exceed the minimal profit on the new order. When the chief engineer found out about the problem (i.e. the business people had a talk with him), he thought for some minutes then simply taped over the logo part of the mould and 'hey presto', nameless soles for a fraction of a dollar!

In 1998 a marketing manager was having problems with the enormous costs of printing and distribution of foreign-language catalogues, after an over-run meeting he went to the near-deserted works canteen, where the only other occupant was an IT worker. Remarking upon how worried the marketing person looked the marketing person poured out his problem to which the IT man suggested customers could download the catalogues from the website. This illustrates that innovation is time and context dependent – downloads in the travel branch in 1998 was an enormous leap and indeed helped the organization involved to be over-proportionally profitable for several years.

Another case study reported by Greenberg and Baron (2000) concerns Timothy Koogle, the founder of Yahoo, who argues that the web portal owes its success to the idea that all employees should communicate freely with each other. Surely this is more support for the idea of 'diversity innovation'?

Examples are numerous but the idea of diversity innovation is about being nimble and flexible so the company can add value and service its customers without 'having to re-invent the wheel'.

Utterback (1994) showed that companies often start with a 'product innovation'. In this work, product innovation maps to 'invention innovation', or as is more common in the case in SMEs, 'creativity innovation'. After the introduction of the product to the market, Utterback (1994) shows that the impact of the 'product innovation' grows less, and 'process innovation' becomes more important (Figure 3.2). That consists mostly of 'diversity innovation'. An example is the invention of the light bulb, a great breakthrough masterminded by Thomas Edison (1847–1931) but where the first light bulbs were rather expensive because they were produced by craftsmen and using a process involving many hundreds of steps: Clearly 'process innovation' (here in relation to SMEs referred to as 'diversity innovation', although other types of innovation may be involved) was an important factor in automating this process so as to ensure that satisfactory light bulbs could be produced at an acceptable price.

Diversity innovation, however, is more than production innovation, because diversity innovation encompasses not only technical improvements, but also improvements in business models, marketing and many other areas. Analogously to Utterback's model, the majority of SMEs could be imagined as sitting on the right-hand curve, perhaps in the supply chain of larger primary innovators. Thus how they lever diversity innovation in an entrepreneurial sense (i.e. to make or discover new and more efficient value chains) is of primary importance in their survival.

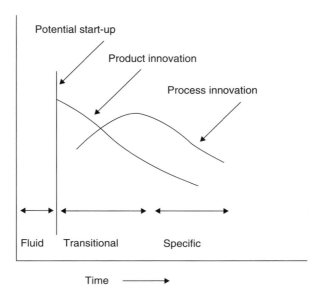

Figure 3.2 **Change in type of innovation with time.**

Note: Ideas in a 'fluid' phase crystallize into an innovative product. If appropriate, a company can be set up at this point. However the effect of product innovation decreases and the focus shifts to process innovation in a transitory stage. Eventually the two curves come closer and parallel, the so-called 'specific phase'. Modified from Utterback (1994).

3.3   Correlating different typologies

The architecture of innovation management was originally proposed by Henderson and Clark (1990). Briefly, radical innovation is an intellectual jump, which changes a whole area. An example of this is the steam engine of the 1770s, which revolutionized industrial production, resulting in the price of cotton cloth falling to 0.1% of what it had been. Vertical innovation reflects the mobility of ideas at a systems level, i.e. between the social strata of a society.

It can be seen from Figure 3.1 that diversity innovation accounts for most innovation, and from Figure 3.3 that diversity innovation is prominent in quadrant H/I but also significantly present in quadrants V/I and H/R. Some authors refer to the '4Ps of innovation', Product, Process, Position and Paradigm (note that this is not the same as Kotlers '4Ps of Marketing', see Kotler & Armstrong, 1989), and some authors even construct 3D relationships. In principle, vertical can refer to Paradigm and the assembly line example above to the process part and perhaps the motor engine to the product part. However it can be seen that mapping the two systems onto each other is not concrete and indeed the 4P model suffers from being rather blurred, especially with respect to services.

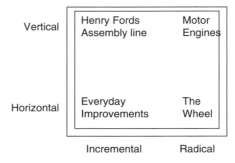

	Incremental	Radical
Vertical	Henry Fords Assembly line	Motor Engines
Horizontal	Everyday Improvements	The Wheel

Figure 3.3   **Types of innovation.**

Note: Matrix showing some examples of vertical and horizontal innovation, and incremental/radical innovation (taken from Mellor, 2005b).

3.4   How do innovations spread?

The major works on the spread of innovations are E. M. Rogers' book *Diffusion of Innovations* (often called DoI theory, originally published in 1962, but most often referred to in the 3rd edition, published in 1983) and expanded upon by Davis (1989) in his 'Technology Acceptance Model', which is especially relevant for IT and even today may help explain e.g. the penetration of Internet marketing.

To borrow an analogy from chemistry; lightweight molecules or atoms vibrating or moving with a high energy (ideas) are introduced into a population of other molecules or atoms. Clearly they interact with many of these, donating, by collision, energy to the recipient. The recipient molecules are thus also imparted movement. However the recipient population is heterogeneous, thus recipient molecules or atoms may be moved more (or less) according to their molecular or atomic mass. Some are able to move very fast (in DoI parlance, early adopters), while at the other extreme there may be those who move only sluggishly (in DoI parlance, laggards). Some of those who, early on, absorb high levels of energy, may bounce into laggards and help speed them up (in DoI parlance, change agents).

DoI theory states that the stages through which a technological innovation passes are:

1. knowledge (exposure to its existence, and understanding of its functions);
2. persuasion (the forming of a favourable attitude to it);
3. decision (commitment to its adoption);
4. implementation (putting it to use); and
5. confirmation (reinforcement based on positive outcomes from it).

Early adopters are generally more highly educated, have a higher social status, are more open to both mass media and interpersonal channels of communication, and have more contact with change agents. It is a generally accepted dogma that mass media channels are relatively more important at the knowledge stage, whereas interpersonal channels are relatively more important at the persuasion stage. Important characteristics of an innovation include:

- relative advantage (the degree to which it is perceived to be better than what it supersedes);
- compatibility (consistency with existing values, past experiences and needs);
- complexity (difficulty of understanding and use);
- trial ability (the degree to which it can be experimented with on a limited basis);
- observability (the visibility of its results).

Different adopter categories exist according to their adoption on a developmental time scale. Classically the time scale used is correlated with overall use, on a Bass Curve (see Mahajan et al. 1990. For a more recent review of developments, see Bass, 2004). The shape of the curve, where N is the number of adopters at time t, is given by the formula:

$$N_t = N_{t-1} + p\,(m - N_{t-1}) + \frac{q\,N_{t-1}\,(m - N_{t-1})}{m}$$

Equation 3.1: The common formula for establishing a Bass curve.

The three parameters used in the equation are:

- m = the market potential; the total number of people who will eventually use the product
- p = the coefficient of external influence; the likelihood that somebody who is not yet using the product will start using it because of mass media coverage or other external factors
- q = the coefficient of internal influence; the likelihood that somebody who is not yet using the product will start using it because of 'word-of-mouth' or other influence from those already using the product.

The standard Bass curve, which normally uses average values of p and q of 0.03 and 0.38, respectively. In plain terms this means that if you need a service or product (i.e. you are a potential adopter) and a trusted person recommended one, then there is a 1:3 chance that you will use that service or product. In graphical form this looks like the curve presented in Figure 3.4:

Other forms of presentation are therefore also known. That which probably has the widest acceptance is plotting, not the degree of acceptance, but the number of adopters, against time on a Bell (or 'Gauss') curve. This has the added

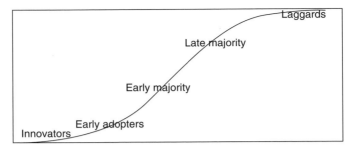

Figure 3.4 **A hypothetical Bass curve illustrating the spread of an innovation among a population with time. Please note that achieving 100% refers to 100% of all adopters, not 100% of the general population.**

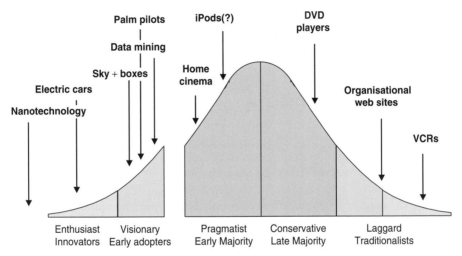

Figure 3.5 *The high-tech adoption curve, illustrating the 'innovation chasm' (Moore, 1995). While this Probability Density Function is a popular and graphic illustration of the 'innovation chasm', it is a transformation of a Cumulative Distribution Function (i.e. a Gauss curve) and not a Bass curve. Thus it is, at best, an approximation (and at worst, misleading) regarding the area under the curve (i.e. the numbers of individuals in each segment). Reproduced by permission of David Wells, Royal Holloway, University of London.*

advantage of clearly illustrating the 'innovation chasm' (Moore, 1995), where the early adopter market becomes saturated before the early majority market takes off.

It is worth repeating here that interpersonal channels are perceived to be relatively more important at the persuasion stage in DoI theory; this corresponds well to the 'Innovation Chasm' (see Figure 3.5) described by Moore (1995). The importance of this highlights the importance of interpersonal relationships – trust – in SMEs, where e.g. technology innovations may arise in the IT deptartment, but fail to spring over the innovation chasm due to lack of interpersonal trust relationships with other departments (or other organizational 'compartments' like overseas offices) in the company (see Chapter 2, section 2.2). In terms of Knowledge Valley Theory, this does not, however, represent a rift in the DI net (see Chapter 6), but is rather a Porterian factor, as it is intimately connected to the nature of the product itself.

3.5 Information gatekeepers

Equation 3.1 and Figure 3.4 show how innovations spread in an open population. It is important to remember that the curve, upon reaching the top right-hand corner, represents 100% of all those individuals who will adopt the innovation and not 100% of the sum of all individuals in a population. For example, in an agricultural subsistence economy, going shopping can be considered an innovation. But in most western economies this innovation (shopping) has spread to almost all individuals, thus in western countries there is a negligible difference between 100% of adopters and 100% of the population. Conversely buying luminous slippers (so you can find them at night) is an innovation where one may expect considerable difference between the total number of adopters (wearers of luminous slippers) and the total number of people in the population.

Thus DoI can be applied to large populations (e.g. the adoption of Internet shopping among the population generally), but it is not applicable in studying the spread of ideas inside small organizations. Indeed, it may not even be applicable to the spread of innovations between different companies, since many simply imitate (Arundel et al. 1995). An example is the banking business; innovative banks started to introduce revolutionary concepts including credit/debit cards, cash vending machines (ATMs) and Internet banking. Each of these innovations exhibited a long lag phase, where proof-of-concept was established. Adoption then spread by imitation of the concept, with extra time lags caused either by conservatism or by the time needed to circumvent proprietary rights on the technology used and so on. Thus adoption was not the theoretical smooth curve like Figures 3.4 and 3.5, but was by a random block-wise process until all banks interested in these systems had adopted them (see Gopalakrishnan & Bierly, 2001).

This becomes an important distinction when considering the spread of innovations between departments inside and within organizations; one assumes that an innovation arising in one department fills it up, like water in a cistern, until some kind of overflow decants it off into the next cistern or department, whereupon this process repeats itself. The knowledge overflow mechanism could also be called the 'information gatekeeper'.

The information gatekeeper is often the departmental manager. If the 'knowledge waters' reach the departmental manager – i.e. if 100% of adopters of the innovation represent close to 100% of the population of that department – then one hopes the manager will function as an effective information gateway and will be able to pass on the knowledge about the existence of the innovation and what advantages it offers, to other departmental managers, for adoption elsewhere.

However, if the number of adopters is significantly less than the number of employees in that department, then the information gatekeeper may remain ignorant about the existence of the innovation, or may dismiss it as inconsequential. Thus the information gatekeeper must be a sympathetic change agent, keeping a sharp eye out for any innovations that even only a few employees use. Change agents (as defined by DoI theory) are extremely important because when innovation comes from outside the dominant group, traditional change agents such as supporting executives may feel treated as unworthy and actually become resistance agents (Kirton, 2003, p.295). This is important because it can lead to 'guileful behaviour' (Williamson, 1995) which in turn may lead to the negation of the basic assumptions of Transaction Cost Theory – finally ending up working diametrically against the organization's best interests. Similarly 'turf wars' between leaders of rival departments are against the organization's best interests, as well as hindering the spread of innovations. Either way, the failure of information gatekeepers to recognize innovations, or their failure to pass recognized innovations on to others (perhaps due to lack of interpersonal trust relationships with other departments, see Chapter 2, section 2.2) may have a catastrophic effect on whole-company innovation and therefore performance. Since information gatekeepers are 'only' human, it is perhaps wisest to assume that while DoI theory can be applied to e.g. the acceptance of an innovative product among consumers (i.e. spreading in 'borderless' containers due to Brownian motion), but it is probably prudent to assume that it is not truly applicable to the spread of workplace innovations in organizations, either as 'pure' DoI, or in a 'cistern and overflow' version, due to narrow compartmentalization.

36 3

GENERAL INTRODUCTION • INTRODUCTION TO KNOWLEDGE MANAGEMENT • **INTRODUCTION TO INNOVATION** • INTRODUCTION TO ENTREPRENEURSHIP • INTRODUCTION TO SMES • CONSTRUCTING KNOWLEDGE VALLEY • MANAGING FORMAL KNOWLEDGE • USING KVT TO IDENTIFY INNOVATION

GENERAL INTRODUCTION • INTRODUCTION TO KNOWLEDGE MANAGEMENT • CTION TO INNOVATION•INTRODUCTION TO ENTREPRENEURSHIP•INTRODUCTION • CONSTRUCTING KNOWLEDGE VALLEY • MANAGING FORMAL KNOWLEDGE • USING KVT TO IDENTIFY INNOVATION BOOSTING FACTORS • FACTORS THAT STOP INNOVATION • A SUMMARY OF LESSONS LEARNT FROM KVT • RECOMBINING KNOWLEDGE AND LEARNING PROVOKES INSPIRATION • SOME CONCLUSIONS AND SUMMING UP • CHOOSING POSSIBLE TECHNOLOGIES • CALCULATE YOUR BENEFIT • LARGER ORGANIZATIONS

4 introduction to entrepreneurship

By the beginning of the twentieth century, neoclassical economics had refined the theory of the capitalist economy to one where the central concept is market equilibrium, and where market supply equals demand in a perfectly competitive market. In this scheme there is little place for innovative entrepreneurs. Interestingly, Marxist theoreticians also belittled entrepreneurs as merely being factors adding to the 'background noise' in the grand historical imperative. The benefits of economies of scale, i.e. the supremacy of the large corporation, remained the dominant theory (see e.g. Galbraith, 1967) for much of the century. However several scholars, the most prominent being Schumpeter, insisted that the equilibrium could be radically disturbed by the introduction of innovative products or services. In this, though, Schumpeter received relatively little recognition.

Classically, economics recognizes three factors in production, raw materials, labour and capital. All products, both goods and services, are a mixture of these three components. Value is created by combining them in such a way that human needs can be satisfied. Since the industrial revolution this process has taken place in organizations. Under these circumstances, entrepreneurship is sometimes referred to as the fourth factor, the way of organizing the other three factors. Thus entrepreneurship (classically) means:

1. Finding new products or combinations in order to satisfy needs (to innovate).
2. Organize resources effectively (to create organizations).
3. Create wealth by adding value (to generate employment).

The word entrepreneur comes from the French 'entre' meaning 'between'. The root of the verb *entreprendre* can be traced back to around 1200 but as language evolves this has caused confusion between the concept of a 'middle man' or intermediary (the 'between' part) on one hand, and on the other hand, the concept of an innovative businessperson using superior managerial ability, new and improved methods, etc., to achieve commercial growth.

As a broad generalization, classical economics focuses on the creation of demand, then satisfying this with a slightly lower supply (i.e. reaping Ricardian profits, or 'rents'). This is in contrast to an entrepreneur, who today would be described as a person who uses innovative methods to restructure a value chain so as to reap an entrepreneurial (or Schumpeterian) profit.

Entrepreneurship is a topic largely overlooked in classical economics and indeed Schumpeter (e.g. 1939, 1942) is hardly mentioned in the standard textbooks, probably because entrepreneurship is not particularly amenable to mathematical modelling, and thus is often regarded by academics as, at the most, an interesting exception to neoclassical economic theory. However, Joseph A. Schumpeter introduced entrepreneurship theory and practice and Schumpeter's book *Theorie der wirtschaftlichen Entwicklung* (1912) directed the attention of economists away from static systems and towards economic advancement. As many authors including Mellor (2008) point out, Schumpeterian rents are those arising from innovation, they are by their nature dynamic and transitory, and occur in the time between the initial innovation and the rise of imitation. Nevertheless, they may generate high returns for considerable periods of time. Entrepreneurship has been a recognized as an independent discipline of management science in the USA since 1987 and since 2000 in the UK.

4.1 The classical works and concepts

Later, Schumpeter (1939) also popularized the work of Nikolai Kondratieff. Kondratieff (1935) developed the theory that technology stimulates industries in waves lasting approximately 50 to 60 years (the 'Kondratieff Cycle'). Each cycle consists of around 20 years to perfect and use a series of related technologies, followed by 20 years where the growth industries appear to be doing well, but what looks like record profits are actually repayments on capital in industries that have ceased to grow. This perilous situation can turn to crisis, often precipitated by a relatively minor panic, and crash. There follows a long period of stagnation during which new, emergent technologies cannot generate enough jobs to make the economy grow again. Completed Kondratieff Cycles include the 'steam & agriculture' cycle (1820–70), 'rail & coal & steel & textile' cycle (1870–1930) and the 'electrical & auto & rubber & petroleum' cycle (1930–80).[1] Kondratieff also indicated that due to progression considerations the contents of previous cycles couldn't be repeated, thus earning himself execution at the hands of Stalin, who had just instigated an 'agricultural renewal' in the USSR.

In the 1960s, uncertainty among the 'smokestack' industries led to widespread diversification among large companies. The strategy was that if you had a finger

---

[1] The cycle beginning in 1980 has variously been postulated to be 'IT & Internet', 'banking & finance' or 'bio/nano/space technology'. I personally believe that the bio/nano/space technology' cycle has yet to come, but we will probably have to wait 40 years to find out what the present cycle really is!

in many pies, then nothing much could go wrong. This went so far that many giant corporations ended up with divisions in rubber, in electronics, in chemicals, in steel, in coal and so on. However it soon became obvious that quite different sets of skills were needed to profitably run each division. This led to a process of divestment, where the new mentality dictated: 'do what you are good at'. This shift meant that each industry had quite a narrow focus. It was built on the assumption that there only are a certain number of industries and that therefore understanding and controlling these will lead to optimal performance (for review see e.g. Mellor, 2003a, 2005a). Many scholars believe that this break-up of markets – the so-called 'post Fordist era' – was actually the natural result of the downswing in the last Kondratieff cycle (Kondratieff, 1935), which introduced a period of 'creative destruction' (Schumpeter, 1942). This process has cast new light on the role of the entrepreneur, the force that rearranges the market into new and more efficient forms (e.g. Drucker, 1985).

The works of Schumpeter and Kondratieff were popularized by Peter F. Drucker, for example in his influential text *Innovation and Entrepreneurship* (1985). Drucker contrasted the employment situation in Europe and in the USA, because at that time the USA was booming, while Europe showed the symptoms of being at the stagnation end of a Kondratieff cycle. While there could be little doubt that the western economy had entered the 'post Fordist' stage (the end of the 'smokestack' industries and beginning of the 'sunrise' industries), Drucker argued that the difference was due to the entrepreneurial culture in the USA, which was more flexible and thus better able to take advantage of the change. The effect was that within five years most European governments (and the EU itself) had passed legislation setting up initiatives to promote innovation and entrepreneurship.

4.2   What it's all about: Improving the value chain

The IT and Internet revolution of the late 1990s again focussed attention on the possibilities of opening up new business areas, it showed that – against existing dogma – it was possible to make new business where there no previous industry or business existed; the so-called 'sunrise' industries (e.g. Microsoft). However it also cast just as much attention on the fact that existing business process can be recombined to form new 'value chains', involving the faster delivery of products that were both better and cheaper.

This is the basis of entrepreneurship theory; innovation and entrepreneurship are often associated with the terms 'value chain' and 'creative destruction' (note that disruptions, discontinuities and disintermediations are for companies, and that end customers should experience progress, not disruptions). The value chain

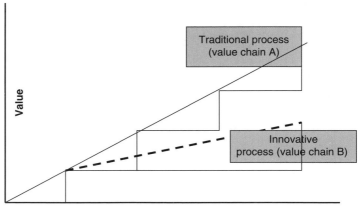

Value

Traditional process
(value chain A)

Innovative
process (value chain B)

Progression towards final market

Figure 4.1 **In traditional processes, value is added in a series of steps; as illustrated by 'value chain A' a company may e.g. make pig iron from iron ore (the first triangle) then sell their product on the next, who may make steel, then sell their product on the next, who may make steel sheets, then sell their product on the next, who may press sheet steel to car bodies, then sell their product on the next, who may make automobiles. This is classically the realm of Input–Output Economics (i.e. that one persons output is the next persons input) and the value (e.g. as price per kilo) increases as one progresses along the links of the value chain. In value chain B innovation (e.g. a new smelting or cheaper rolling process, or novel materials) is used to construct a new value chain. The old intermediaries are stranded ('creative destruction') while the entrepreneurial innovator can vary the final height of the stippled line to share more or less of his 'Schumpetrian rents' with the final customer. Taken from Mellor (2008) and reprinted with permission of Sage Publishers.**

represents the value of a product in an unfinished state and increasing in value as it reaches the customer. The expression 'value chain' is also used in an intra-organizational sense, referring to a bundle of factors affecting value, from when a product enters the firm, to when it leaves it. Several 'value chains' may make up a 'value system' (see Porter, 1990). Disruptions or discontinuities in the value chain cause a disturbance in the manufacturing or marketing equilibrium, leaving previous processes or intermediaries out-manoeuvred, stranded outside the value chain, abandoned and bankrupt. This is referred to as 'creative destruction'.

GENERAL INTRODUCTION • INTRODUCTION TO KNOWLEDGE MANAGEMENT •
CTION TO INNOVATION•INTRODUCTION TO ENTREPRENEURSHIP•INTRODUCTION
• CONSTRUCTING KNOWLEDGE VALLEY • MANAGING FORMAL KNOWLEDGE • USING
KVT TO IDENTIFY INNOVATION BOOSTING FACTORS • FACTORS THAT STOP INNOVATION
• A SUMMARY OF LESSONS LEARNT FROM KVT • RECOMBINING KNOWLEDGE AND
LEARNING PROVOKES INSPIRATION • SOME CONCLUSIONS AND SUMMING UP • CHOOSING
POSSIBLE TECHNOLOGIES • CALCULATE YOUR BENEFIT • LARGER ORGANIZATIONS

5 Introduction to SMEs

The title of this book includes the term 'growing organizations'. Organizations almost always start – at new venture formation – by being small and then if successful they grow. The smaller section of the organization spectrum are called SMEs – Small and Medium-sized Enterprises. SMEs are not a main focus of this book but they are highly relevant to the economy and thus to Knowledge Management. Indeed many implementations of Information Systems will be in an SME environment and will be expressly aimed at helping such an organization grow. Thus in this section the developmental taxonomy of companies will briefly be discussed, from founding as fledgling start-ups, to companies with over 200 employees. The EU Report on the implementation of the European Charter for Small Enterprises (2005) states that in the EU: 'Small businesses play a central role in the European economy. Some 25 million small businesses, constituting 99% of all businesses, employ almost 95 million people, providing 55% of total jobs in the private sector'.

5.1 Classifications of companies

Companies differ wildly in their size and aims and this underlines the need to classify companies into meaningful groups. These categories, however, are fluid; clearly a hairdresser employing nine people would be a large company by hairdresser standards. Similarly a company with 240 employees would be considered small if it were a foundry or shipyard. Eurosat defines companies according to their number of employees as shown in Table 5.1. In 1996, however, the European Union (EU) revised the lower border for large organizations from 500 down to 250. The modified Eurosat definition is presented here, despite differing from the current US definition (still 500). However there is little agreement on exact borders between the categories, e.g. in the UK the British Bank Association defines small firms as having an annual turnover of under 1 million pounds (i.e. not number of employees at all), while the Companies Act defines small firms as having an annual turnover of under 2.8 million pounds.

Table 5.1 **A classification of companies: An example of one possible scheme for classifying companies according to size (number of employees).**

Designation	Number of employees
Micro-organizations	1–9 employees
Small-organizations	10–99 employees
Medium sized organizations	100–249 employees
Large-organizations	250+ employees

It can be seen that, according to the definition used here (table 5.1), SMEs range from 10 to 249 employees. However micro-organizations (1–9) are often included, as the borders are quite fuzzy (e.g. a market garden company may employ 6 permanent staff and 20 seasonal labourers). Additionally, some authors add a further category of very large organizations, with over 1000 employees. This is quite sensible because the behaviour of such companies (often multinational companies) is quite different from purely national large companies, e.g. the majority of patent applications come from these very large companies. However it is important, when looking at the contribution of SMEs to employment, to realize that statistics can be quite misleading, e.g. if a company employing 200 persons expands by 25%, it moves over into the large firm category, and the statistics will show a net loss of 200 jobs in the SME category, and a gain of 250 in the large company category.

To give some impression of the importance of SMEs to the national economy; guesstimates at the time of going to press range around the figure of 3.5 million SMEs in the UK, as opposed to approx 7000 large companies.

Existing small and medium sized companies have also been subjected to different kinds of classification, e.g. those of Birch (1987) and Storey (1994). These are summarized in Table 5.2.

Please note that Storey (1994) also mentions a third type, 'failures'. This may well correspond to 'pseudo-entrepreneurial companies' in the Covin & Slevins scheme as in Table 5.3. The difference between the above classifications and Covin & Slevins scheme is that the above classifications put companies into rigid categories and do not account for development. Covin & Slevin (Covin & Slevin, 1998; Slevin & Covin, 1990) propose a different taxonomy based on management style versus organizational structure and they note that companies can swing between these categories.

While not wishing to propose a completely new taxonomy, I believe that in addition to the above, organizations with zero employees should also be included, as that represents a person with a regular job who runs a company in their spare time. The theory presented later – Knowledge Valley Theory – would also argue for a classification up to 50 employees because that is where the growth barrier

42 5

GENERAL INTRODUCTION • INTRODUCTION TO KNOWLEDGE MANAGEMENT • INTRODUCTION TO INNOVATION • INTRODUCTION TO ENTREPRENEURSHIP • **INTRODUCTION TO SMES** • CONSTRUCTING KNOWLEDGE VALLEY • MANAGING FORMAL KNOWLEDGE • USING KVT TO IDENTIFY INNOVATION

Table 5.2 *Classification of companies: An example of one possible scheme for classifying companies according to knowledge use and market development.*

Name (Birch, 1987)	Name (Storey, 1994)	Knowledge intensive	Type of market
Elephants	–	Rarely	Mature
Mice	Trundler	Almost never	Mature
Gazelles	Flyer	Often	Immature

Table 5.3 *Classification of companies: An example of one possible scheme for classifying companies according to according to dominant managerial type and administrative structure (a 'Covin & Slevin' classification).*

	Flexible structure	Rigid or mechanistic structure
Entrepreneurial Management	Effective entrepreneurial companies. These companies are effective because their structure enhances communication and minimizes bureaucratic barriers to innovation.	Pseudo-entrepreneurial companies. The lack of flexibility means that innovation will not flourish, or will not be applied. These companies are ineffective.
Conservative Management	Unstructured-unadventurous companies. These firms have the ability to respond quickly to opportunities, but are best at providing customized, non-standard output.	Efficient-bureaucratic companies. These companies are successful because they operate in environments where customers require standardized, uniform products or services. Such companies can often compete on price alone.

imposed by the mathematics of diversity innovation begins to bite (see Chapter 6, section 6.1.2).

However, brush my thoughts aside and instead to go into details of the most-used (Birch, 1987), classification:

- Elephants are larger, slow-growing companies that are relatively stable and unresponsive to changes in the economy. They are unlikely to have more than one patent or other protection (invention innovation) like trademarks, and may well use a focused form of creativity. They are unlikely to use, or permit the use of, diversity innovation and may tend towards conservative management structures.
- Mice are small, often family, low-growth firms that 'reproduce' rapidly. In the USA there may be a million such firms newly registered each year. They

use neither invention nor diversity innovation, but may be rather creative in sensing new business opportunities in already-established (mature) markets. Because they may be so small it may be misleading to speak of a management structure.

- Gazelles are new ventures, sometimes, but not always, centred on a small core of invention innovation, thus they are often by definition in immature – new and expanding – markets. They may be creative and, due to their size and market, are also able to lever diversity innovation, especially in the fields of IT and biotechnology. Their management style is likely to be entrepreneurial.

5.2 SME development

Which kind of company is started and how it develops, is largely dependant upon the personal wishes of the owner/entrepreneur involved. Similarly the owner/entrepreneur may wish to explore an immature market, or may wish to inhabit a niche in a mature market (or even challenge the market leaders). These are all perfectly valid personal choices. Alternatively and from the point of view of an investor, putting money into e.g. an elephant that inhabits a niche in a mature market may be preferable to investing in an immature market and hoping the risky hope that the investment object turns out to be a gazelle.

Starting up and running a company is, for the majority of owner/entrepreneurs, a highly personal vehicle for some kind of self-realization. The basic choices for a prospective entrepreneur are what targets are meant to be reached. First, the original idea may take the venture into an immature market, or into a niche in an established (mature) market. Furthermore, very few prospective entrepreneurs will go all-out for a growth company in a consequent manner. Very early the strategic choice has to be made regarding ambition niveau; a large portion of a small cake, or a small portion of a large cake? Clearly going for the large cake (being growth oriented) will entail selling most of the company, behaving in a consequent, logical and responsible manner, borrowing large amounts of money and will include bowing to the will of the majority of directors or stockholders. Many owner/entrepreneurs have no desire to act as if they were employees, and prefer to rule their own small kingdom as they see fit. Thus these SMEs will often deviate widely from the rules of good financial management as epitomized by e.g. Transaction Cost Theory (Williamson, 1995, Williamson and Masten, 1999) and will not be growth-oriented. Furthermore, the daily running of such companies can be erratic, as the owner/entrepreneur lays most value on advice from close acquaintances and family, all of who may be lacking in leadership skills (although no reflection on their management skills, the most famous example of a family business is probably the Ahlstrom Corp. of Finland, which Magretta (1998)

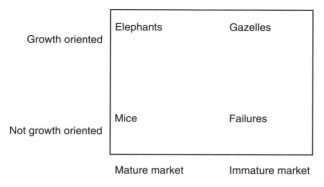

Figure 5.1 **Possible consequences of strategy on SME outcome. This model shows the tendencies in SMEs as a result of the owner/entrepreneur choice about growth versus personal control, as affected by the maturity of the market foreseen.**

reported employs 200 family members). This pattern becomes established when staff, especially management staff, begin to be employed.

Psychologists agree that in situations where it is possible, people will decide to be together with others who share the same point of view. Being part of such a consensus group makes living much pleasanter (Kirton, 2003). The consequence is that the SME owner/entrepreneurs (and indeed many managers) surround themselves with people who agree with them and share similar cultural and knowledge bases, and may avoid those individuals who come with thorny logical and rational arguments that contradict the 'leader view'. These are ideal conditions for nurturing a management innovation gap (similar to that described in Figure 3.5 for product innovation), and certainly does not help leaders to act as good information gatekeepers and change agents, thus helping stifle much-needed innovation. How can this affect the developmental trajectory of a company?

Clearly some companies start small and grow larger and indeed there are several developmental models of company growth; the most often cited are Greiner (1972) and Churchill and Lewis (1983), as well as Garnsey (1996). These and others are adequately reviewed in the standard literature (e.g. Kirby, 2003; Mellor, 2003a). The static stage/age model of small business development describes six stages as given in Table 5.4:

The six stage model of small business development describes a hypothetical model for the evolution of an SME through its lifetime, however their developmental trajectories differ (Table 5.5). Most new ventures fail. Those that survive clearly have some kind of viable mercantile activity. Generally speaking the life cycle of a commercial company is similar to the Product Life Cycle concept where the company will grow, become mature and wane. Churchill and Lewis (1983) sketched out the different kinds of leadership a firm gets as it progresses

*Table 5.4 **Developmental stages in the life cycle of a company: The psychological and cultural drivers predominant in the leadership consensus group (Kirton, 2003) throughout the major phases from founding to decline.***

Name	Characteristic
Existence	Staying alive by finding or developing products or services and attracting customers
Survival	Establishing a customer base and demonstrating viability
Success	Confidence in a market position and the emergence of options for further growth
Take-off	Opting to go for growth
Maturity	Exhibiting the characteristics of a larger and stable company
Decline	Overconfidence or 'milking strategy', possibly dominating a shrinking market, products are reaching the end of their life cycle.

*Table 5.5 **Stages in the development of a hypothetical company. The term 'hockey stick' is explained in Figure 6.9. Please note that Churchill and Lewis terminology focuses on the stages up to maturity whereas others (indicated by an 'M') continue through to the end of the life cycle and even consider regeneration or renewal.***

Stage	Churchill and Lewis terminology	Mellor terminology	Type of manager needed
1 –	Conception and existence	The startup stage	Adventurer
2 (Churchill and Lewis terminology)	Survival	–	–
3 (Churchill and Lewis terminology)	Profitability and stabilization	–	–
4 –	Profitability and growth	The hockey-stick stage	Warrior
5 (Churchill and Lewis terminology)	Take off	–	–
6 –	Maturity	The professional stage	Hunter
4 M	–	Mature and Consolidating stage	Farmer
5 M	–	The declining stage	Politician
6 M	–	The sustaining stage	Turnaround (Visionary)

through its life cycle. Variations in terminology are common and as an example I have taken one of my models (Mellor, 2003a, 2003b) as a comparison, but others equally valid can be found without any difficulty.

Interestingly the earlier work by Greiner (1972) describes growth through five stages of relatively clam 'evolution' where the transition to the subsequent stage is characterized by a chaotic 'revolution'. Greiner's stages are (Table 5.6):

Table 5.6 **The Greiner (1972) model stages as applied to growth-oriented SMEs. Please note that if success at crisis Stage 5 (i.e. renewal) is not chosen then further options include divestment or break-up into a group of smaller enterprises.**

Greiner stage	Characteristics of the evolutionary stage	Followed by revolution	
1	Creativity	Crisis of leadership	Moving from purely entrepreneurial drive to leadership that has different specialist knowledge
2	Direction	Crisis of autonomy	Line staff need to decide between procedures and initiative
3	Delegation	Crisis of control	Lower and middle managers are perceived to have excess power and there is little cross-talk between divisions
4	Coordination	Crisis of red tape	Senior management has adopted a watch-dog approach
5	Collaboration	Crisis of psychological saturation	Shift to interpersonal collaboration to get employees to work together through a sense of mission or purpose.

The weakness with the Greiner (1972) model is that it correlates the age of a company with its size, but does not specify any units. That is not so tragic where age is concerned because some companies may simply be moving slower, but the units regarding size are critical if one is to apply business information systems to ameliorating the crisis periods.

5.3 Deploying information systems in the SME area

In Chapter 6 we will talk about Knowledge Valley Theory. This theory is integral to the application of organization-wide Information Systems, providing employees with deeper understanding on the business processes but also attenuating stress and improving innovation with cross-fertilization of ideas and just-in-time knowledge. As shown in Table 5.6, Greiner (1972) is actually providing us with an un-calibrated map as to where business Information Systems can best be applied. As we will see in the next chapter, Knowledge Valley Theory applies to all organizations of whatever size (although limits to computational power presently restrict this to enterprises with from 0 to between 200 and 249 employees). However looking at Figure 6.12 one can see that there are crises at employee number 40–50 and again at 80–100. If these two crises correspond to Greiner stages 1 and 2 (which appears to be an unsubstantiated but reasonable suggestion), then one could put the magic missing figures on the Greiner model. Especially stage two – which would also correspond to the Churchill and Lewis stages around stage 4 and are known to be particularly vital – agrees with the harrowing financial risk and consequences predicted for this point (employee number 90–110) by Knowledge Valley Theory and shown in Figure 6.14.

How does this help us in using information systems to further organizational aims? Well, although Knowledge Valley Theory applies to all organizations, those under a size of 40–50 employees are unlikely to have heard of it, unlikely to use it and indeed are unlikely to think it relevant to them (which may be correct, if the owner decides his company is not going to be growth-oriented). However the next stages are interesting. To recap, stages 3–5 are:

3. Lower and middle managers (i.e. information gatekeepers) are perceived to have excess power and there is little cross-talk between divisions.
4. Senior management has adopted a watchdog approach.
5. Shift to interpersonal collaboration to get employees to work together through a sense of mission or purpose.

If this is not ringing a bell then go to jail, do not pass go and do not collect £200! These are exactly the problems that Business-oriented Information Systems are supposed to address, opening information gateways, improve (nay, force!) cross-talk between divisions, automate watchdog mechanisms by means of software and to promote team spirit and thus innovation.

Thus by using the predictions implicit in Knowledge Valley Theory to provisionally calibrate the Greiner (1972) model, we can see that functional business information systems should ideally be put in place in the time when the enterprise is growing over 60–70 employees, that high-risk companies should be equipped for a potentially disastrous transition at around size 90–110 employees and that a mature and fully functioning business-oriented information system is needed at size 110–250 employees. Clearly such systems (as outlined in Chapter 12, section 12.3) are essential as the enterprise extends beyond this size, but Knowledge Valley Theory has reached the present limits of computational power, so we cannot peer into that future with any degree of certainty.

48   5

GENERAL INTRODUCTION • INTRODUCTION TO KNOWLEDGE MANAGEMENT • INTRODUCTION TO INNOVATION • INTRODUCTION TO ENTREPRENEURSHIP • **INTRODUCTION TO SMES** • CONSTRUCTING KNOWLEDGE VALLEY • MANAGING FORMAL KNOWLEDGE • USING KVT TO IDENTIFY INNOVATION

5.4 Peculiarities of the SME area

Finally it is worth noting that an existing company may exist quite happily without an injection of innovation. Innovation is not a pill that will automatically guarantee the recipients good health. Both elephants and larger companies may, for example, be divided into effective departments in order to provide generic basic products (nails, flour, etc.) and may thus be competing basically on price. Assuming that the company possesses the basic competence to keep its production efficient, then innovation will probably only disrupt the smoothly functioning machinery. In such cases it may be wrong to talk about e.g. introducing competing teams into a dynamic and innovative matrix environment etc. Innovation is not unisex, and one size does not fit all! Indeed business-oriented information systems may in such enterprises be reduced to reporting, quality control and statistical software.

The SME area has a reputation for being a chaotic area, with many bankruptcies among under-financed companies in a highly Darwinistic environment. In general SMEs have:

- high mortality rates
- low equity/debt ratio and costly access to sources of finance
- weak market orientation due to lack of specialized expertise
- low productivity leading to high unit labour costs

In this respect there is little difference between most of the EU countries, typically being at the most a difference of 20%, between new VAT registrations and VAT de-registrations. This is often taken as meaning a large churn in the SME population. However again caution must be exercised when interpreting statistics; a VAT deregistration may not mean a business failure, for example business takeovers (where the company being sold deregisters) are successes, as are various other scenarios; e.g. the owner reaching retirement age and selling, the owner having achieved another target and going into voluntary liquidation, or simply a new baby in the house meaning that the owner has to stop and get a 'real job'. All of these are success stories, but they are often classified as failures because they are success stories that cannot be applied to large companies. Similarly SMEs applying for small loans run into transaction cost barriers, because transaction costs are relatively high compared to the small sum being borrowed. Thus, in stark contrast to large companies, SMEs – especially in the UK – often find it cheaper to run on an overdraft (Burns & Whitehouse, 1995).

GENERAL INTRODUCTION • INTRODUCTION TO KNOWLEDGE MANAGEMENT •
O INNOVATION • INTRODUCTION TO ENTREPRENEURSHIP • INTRODUCTION
UCTING KNOWLEDGE VALLEY • MANAGING FORMAL KNOWLEDGE • USING
KVT TO IDENTIFY INNOVATION BOOSTING FACTORS • FACTORS THAT STOP INNOVATION
• A SUMMARY OF LESSONS LEARNT FROM KVT • RECOMBINING KNOWLEDGE AND
LEARNING PROVOKES INSPIRATION • SOME CONCLUSIONS AND SUMMING UP • CHOOSING
POSSIBLE TECHNOLOGIES • CALCULATE YOUR BENEFIT • LARGER ORGANIZATIONS

Part II modelling the theory

Context and aims

The previous chapters introduced some relevant aspects of Knowledge Management, Innovation and Entrepreneurship as separate entities. In this chapter the strands connecting Knowledge Management, Innovation and Entrepreneurship are brought together to form the basis of Knowledge Valley Theory.

The guiding principle is that having established that by skimming other relevant theories, that some are more important than others. In the following we will endeavour to establish an overarching theory that is testable and explains in abstract terms some of the problems that we are confronted with when trying to grow organizations (i.e. those that are small and wish to grow, as well as those that are larger and wish to be more successful). We do that by constructing a fairly simple mathematical model, that said, the model as described here, demands only simple mathematics. However by establishing this framework we will have built a trellis upon which other ideas can flourish.

At the end of this chapter the reader should be able to understand the abstract principles behind the factors driving knowledge use in an organization.

GENERAL INTRODUCTION • INTRODUCTION TO KNOWLEDGE MANAGEMENT •
CTION TO INNOVATION • INTRODUCTION TO ENTREPRENEURSHIP • INTRODUCTION
• CONSTRUCTING KNOWLEDGE VALLEY • MANAGING FORMAL KNOWLEDGE • USING
KVT TO IDENTIFY INNOVATION BOOSTING FACTORS • FACTORS THAT STOP INNOVATION
• A SUMMARY OF LESSONS LEARNT FROM KVT • RECOMBINING KNOWLEDGE AND
LEARNING PROVOKES INSPIRATION • SOME CONCLUSIONS AND SUMMING UP • CHOOSING
POSSIBLE TECHNOLOGIES • CALCULATE YOUR BENEFIT • LARGER ORGANIZATIONS

6 constructing knowledge valley

In the Knowledge Valley Theory (KVT) model presented in this chapter it is important to be aware that persons are represented as nodes (the number of people is represented by P) and are joined by ties, the number of links or ties between nodes is the Diversity Innovation (DI) number. As the DI number increases the potential for innovation increases. That last bit was important, so I'm going to repeat it again; the DI number is not the amount of knowledge in an organization and not the amount of innovation – it merely represents the potential for the type of small-scale, incremental innovations that were described earlier (Chapter 3) and are thought of as being important in small companies.

Clearly some modelling on linked node networks has been done before (see e.g. Rapoport, 1957), and some even relate networks to value (e.g. Montgomery, 1992; who demonstrated in a semi-quantitative way that weak links correlate to higher salaries and aggregate employment rates). The advantages of KVT are that it is strongly quantitative in terms of commercial performance and that by tweaking the input parameters the effect of factors contributing to economic success can be assessed in a fairly clear manner. In the first simple KVT model the main assumptions are that:

1. A person can have a very large number of ties and that there is no upper limit.
2. All ties are exactly similar and have the same 'weight', quality and importance independent of their length.

Later – after making the simple KVT model – these assumptions will be reviewed in the light of Granovetter's theory on the spread of information in social networks known as 'the strength of weak ties' (Granovetter, 1973, 1983, 2004). Briefly, Granovetter explains that:

- there limits to the number of social ties an individual can support,
- that high link (tie) density results in norms and group behaviour,
- that there are three types of tie – absent, weak and strong,
- that weak ties are more likely to carry novel information.

So it can be seen that the 'the strength of weak ties' model is similar to diversity innovation insomuch as strong ties e.g. good daily friendships, rarely represent a diversity of knowledge, whereas passing acquaintanceships give both participants access to novel information, views and experiences. Thus weak ties (acquaintanceships) represent diversity and it is these encounters which are potentially more fruitful.

6.1 The first two dimensions; innovation and employee number

6.1.1 The concept of the DI number

Obviously mutual inspiration cannot take place in isolation. Similarly the concept of diversity innovation needs two or more participants. The isolated individual, illustrated by the rather unflattering circle below, has a diversity innovation number ('DI number') of 0 (Figure 6.1):

*Figure 6.1 **The DI number of an individual when the number of individuals = 1, then the number of communication pathways = 0 (i.e. DI = 0).***

Clearly, when two individuals enter into a communicative relationship, then a communication pathway (sometimes called a link or 'tie') opens, i.e. the DI number reaches 1 (Figure 6.2).

*Figure 6.2 **The DI number of a pair when the number of individuals = 2, then the number of communication pathways = 1 (i.e. DI = 1).***

To expand this concept, as long as the number of people involved is larger than three, then the number of pathways is related to the number of people involved and this relationship can be expressed mathematically by a simple equation: If DI (the Diversity Innovation number) is the number of two-way potential communication pathways and P stands for the number of people involved (often called 'nodes'), then:

$$DI = \frac{P * [P-1]}{2}$$

Equation 6.1: Deriving the DI number (the number of communication pathways) from the number of individuals involved. Note that * is the mathematical symbol for multiply.

Let us pick P to be the number 6. Plugging this into Equation 6.1 results in the number 15 (Figure 6.3). Those with patience can easily check this on the following illustration:

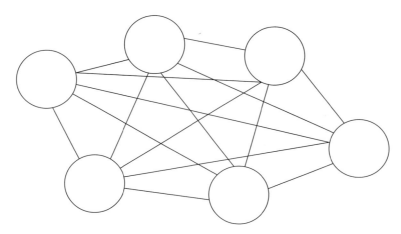

Figure 6.3 **The DI numbers with many nodes when people (P) = 6, then the number of two-way communication pathways = 15 (i.e. DI = 15).**

However it is obvious that for larger numbers, it is much more convenient to use the equation, rather than draw such sketches and count up the number of lines!

Thus we can look at the potential amount of DI throughout the growth of an organization, using Equation 6.1. To do this we will, for the sake of simplicity, start with the absolute nexus; one individual (i.e. DI = 0) who, having just started, has a turnover of 0. Clearly this does not represent all start-ups but this is allowable because we are looking at the evolution of SMEs and the first individual, usually destined to become the owner/director, is actually the core of the SME. Some may point out that a fledgling company may consist of (say) three individuals and have a value that is either positive ('sweat equity', savings, etc.) or negative (investments, loans etc.). My point is that the origin is the same, but merely that it is the moment of business formation – which is purely technical – that is a variable product of personal choice.

Using Equation 6.1, we can plot the amount of potential DI in an organization as it grows and acquires more employees. This curve, from 0 to 249 nodes (employees) is shown in Figure 6.4.

It is an essential prerequisite to note that at this point we are hypothesising that all DI joins are equally important, i.e. we are ignoring knowledge location,

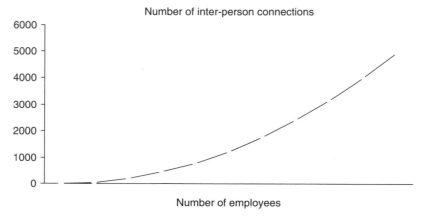

Number of inter-person connections

Number of employees

Figure 6.4 **Increase of DI number with growth of company as expressed by number of employees.**

the ability to share (as well as willingness); the prevention of knowledge attrition through a programme of knowledge definition (codification); knowledge retention; and knowledge transfer. That none withstanding, Figure 6.4 illustrates that the growing firm acquires healthy amounts of DI. Unfortunately, before rubbing our hands in glee, we must consider that there is a downside to this robust growth, namely that communication demands transaction costs.

6.1.2 Growth in DI is limited by the transaction costs for communication

The most obvious transaction cost for communication is simply the time taken to communicate, or rather the opportunity costs associated with spending the time needed to communicate. The transaction costs for communication can be great, as illustrated by the following example:

Case 4

The transaction cost for communication

At the Danish Ministry for Food, Fisheries and Agriculture I was once unfortunately present at a kick-off meeting between a database programmer and an expert in bovine disease who, together with a specialist in animal transport, wanted an Internet based information system made. Before the meeting the veterinarian said they had a 'database' and the transport person reckoned to have a 'program', so the database programmer and I were thus hopeful that the meeting could be concluded within an hour. Unfortunately the veterinarians 'database' turned out to be a stack of handwritten papers, and the transport persons 'program', turned out to be an activity timetable sketched on a large pasteboard. Clearly the

---

computer people – the database programmer and I – had quite different conceptions about what databases and programs[1] are! Thus our prognostication that the
matter could be resolved satisfactorily within an hour was wildly wrong and in fact
the 'experts' inability to express themselves (i.e. communicate) in a clear fashion –
or even to try to adapt a common vocabulary – led to high transaction costs for
communication and in fact this particular project was destined to be exceptionally
tortuous and very time- (and thus money-) consuming.

The transaction costs for communication are still enormously high even in
those cases where all involved 'speak the same language'; e.g. in a company with
120 employees), 7140 communication pathways exit (see Equation 6.1). Taking 5
minutes each, talking continuously and without any break, this would take 595
hours or 16 man-weeks of working time just for employees to talk to each other
for 5 minutes, excluding that any employees got a chance to repeat any conversa-
tions or indeed do any work. Each further employee hired would take 10 man-
hours to talk to existing employees for 5 minutes each. It is these transaction
(& opportunity) costs associated with communication, which are the limiting
factor for diversity (horizontal/incremental) innovation in an SME, or indeed
any other non-SME environment.

No wonder large companies express sentiments like 'if only we knew what we
know'. Even in an enterprise of 249 employees (i.e. still an SME), knowing what
the employees know is truly an impossible task.

The above rough calculation concerns the DI in an organization, i.e. everyone
communicating to everyone else. To get a different perspective let us take just
one individual (e.g. the owner/director) instead. Even speaking briefly to each
employee for 5 minutes will consume 20 hours of his time. That is around 50% to
60% of his working week (depending obviously on how much he works in total).

6.1.3   The transaction cost cut-off point

So where about on the curve (Figure 6.4) is the cut-off point, the point where the
transaction costs for DI become unbearable? Clearly for the individual worker,
the perspective of sitting around doing nothing all day apart from chatting with
his workmates is not unbearable at all, quite the opposite! The 'unbearable' calculation has to be made from the perspective of the cost-bearer: the employer.
Thus the cut-off point will not be one clear-cut, universally applicable dot on the
curve, but rather an area where the cost gradient begins to bite. For example, for
an organization with 50 individuals, at 10 minutes apiece, the boss requires over 8
hours to chat to each of them. This may be just acceptable for some employers, but
sacrificing a whole day a week may already be too much (i.e. too 'expensive') for

---

[1] In my view databases and programs are joined digital tables and compiled executable machine code,
respectively.

many. This cut-off point equates generally to the 'Innovation Chasm' described by Moore (1995) and mentioned in Chapter 3, section 3.4 (see also Figure 3.5). In the Grainer model of SME development (see Chapter 5, section 5.3) it may correspond to the end of stage 1; the 'Crisis of leadership'.

So how do employers cope? Easy: They hire 'sub-employers' to manage this for them. This is the emergence of the middle management in a growing SME and indeed previous work on business growth consulting (Mellor, 2005b) has used this to point out that profound changes in company management structure must occur around company size of 50 employees. It is this challenge, correctly erecting a management structure – often for the first time – which is the largest risk and barrier to further growth.

This point cannot be emphasized too strongly: Table 5.1 showed that the definition of a small-sized enterprise is 9–99 employees, but this is, in fact, grotesquely wrong and indeed misleading because an enterprise of (say) 20 employees has almost no management structure and this is in stark contrast to an enterprise of (say) 80 employees, which has a management structure in place that is both definite and defining. However it is not only that the ends of the supposedly homogeneous division are quite dissimilar, but consider the transition; if they are growth-oriented (i.e. the 'interesting' SMEs, perhaps aiming at Gazelle status) then those enterprises at the lower end will have to inexorably progress to the higher end. Especially the transition from around 40–50 employees to a larger number stresses the organization and requires deep-seated changes in management and leadership. If these are not successfully achieved then the SME will not successfully manage the transition and its growth will be crippled for years. The present nomenclature should therefore be changed (e.g. to small-1 and small-2) to focus the proper and required attention on this make-or-break area.

The transition from 'small' to 'medium', i.e. at size 90–110 employees, is also a highly critical point.

6.1.4 Departmentalization and its consequences for DI

Having established, however, that transaction costs prohibit the growth of the organization as 'one big happy family' above an employee number of around 50, we can proceed to assume that middle management is appointed and that departments, each with a departmental head, are formed. The standard form representing this structure is the organization diagram, or 'organigram'. Figure 6.5 shows a standard example.

There is an adage, derived originally from architecture, that 'form follows function' (e.g. staircases are always similar, since their function is to allow humans to access different levels of a structure). In some molecular science disciplines this has mutated to 'function follows form', i.e. that the structures of molecular catalysts (enzymes etc.) in biology or chemistry are derived from the 3D structures of

GENERAL INTRODUCTION • INTRODUCTION TO KNOWLEDGE MANAGEMENT • INTRODUCTION TO INNOVATION • INTRODUCTION TO ENTREPRENEURSHIP • INTRODUCTION TO SMES • **CONSTRUCTING** **KNOWLEDGE VALLEY** • MANAGING FORMAL KNOWLEDGE • USING KVT TO IDENTIFY INNOVATION

58   6

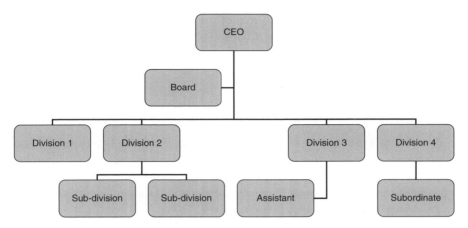

Figure 6.5 **Organization diagram of a hypothetical organization. Standard format taken from Microsoft Office.**

the macromolecule. In business the mutation is even more profound; 'structure follows strategy' (Chandler, 1962) thus the structure of an organization follows the business strategy adopted. Chandler (1962) says that large organizations in the late nineteenth century had a unit arrangement or U-form which allowed a specialized division of labour which in turn promoted economies of scale in production, marketing, distribution and so on. This was then supplanted by the multidivisional or M-form, which released top management from being involved in operational details. Kogut and Zander (1992) argue that historically the next development was to concentrate knowledge and decision-making capabilities to reduce costs while increasing strategic capability.

It is a central thesis of this work that the structure of an organization, an SME, in today's hyper-fragmented markets (Kotler & Trias de Bes, 2003) should reflect the fact that threats and opportunities can come without warning from any angle, thus a 'well rounded', flowing or even amoeboid structure is that which will survive best over more rigid forms. In this form the entrepreneurial team (not just the owner) can anticipate problems and eliminate them before damage can be done. The management of knowledge and intellectual capital contributes markedly (Grant, 1996) towards this end and this view is not only gaining in popularity but also has begun to enter the relevant textbooks (e.g. Besanko et al. 2007). Clearly there is no uniformly 'best' structure for all enterprises in all circumstances and environments, however the rounded sea urchin SME is surprisingly tough, but as growth proceeds this form is no longer tenable and some must become sharks, and some will become sheep.

However, upon acknowledging that the organisms mass has proven too great to remain a sea urchin, the organization must divide into departments. At this point, having partly abandoned 'roundedness' (or at least extreme roundedness) from

BOOSTING FACTORS • FACTORS THAT STOP INNOVATION • A SUMMARY OF LESSONS LEARNT FROM KVT • RECOMBINING KNOWLEDGE AND LEARNING PROVOKES INSPIRATION • SOME CONCLUSIONS AND SUMMING UP • CHOOSING POSSIBLE TECHNOLOGIES • CALCULATE YOUR BENEFIT • LARGER ORGANIZATIONS

6   59

necessity, we can recalculate the DI. Assuming that the DI between departments is one (as given by the organigram), then this is given by the general formula:

$$\frac{[PD*(PD-1)]*D}{2} + \frac{[D*(D-1)\}}{2}$$

Equation 6.2: Deriving the DI number for two departments

Where PD is the number of people in each department and D is the number of departments. This equation assumes that there are at all times an equal number of people in all departments. If the departments are of unequal size then they must be considered separately D number of times and the total summed, i.e. for splitting into 4 uneven departments (so D = 4):

$$\frac{[PD1*(PD1-1)]}{2} + \frac{[PD2*(PD2-1)]}{2} + \frac{[PD3*(PD3-1)]}{2} + \frac{[PD4*(PD4-1)]}{2} + \frac{[4*(4-1)\}}{2}$$

Equation 6.3: Where PD1 is the number of people in department 1, PD2 is the number of people in department 2, department 3 etc.

Table 6.1 shows the effect on DI of forming 6 departments of 10, or 3 departments of 20 (and an unequal split of 50 and 10). Clearly, when the transaction costs of communication become so large as to precipitate dividing the organization on departmental lines, then clever employers will simply split the company into two (or at least as few as possible) departments!

It can be seen from the curves in Figure 6.6 that the effect of forming a departmental structure at all knocks the DI number back to the stone ages: an organization of 60 employees in one big department has a DI of 1770, forming 6 departments of 10 persons each, gives 275, a total DI equivalent to an organization of around 30 people, a decrease of some 74% compared to the theoretical figure without sub-departments. The variable with the largest effect is the number of departments the organization is split into, because the amount of DI in any department is proportional to its size, so fewer departments = larger departments = higher DI.

Please note that the above simple model (Figure 6.6) chops the organization into equally sized departments only, it does not take sub-departments or other further divisions into account (such as those labelled 'sub-department', 'assistant' and

Table 6.1 **The effects on DI number of splitting a company of 60 employees into departments of different sizes.**

	6 depts of 10	3 depts of 20	1 dept of 50 and 1 of 10
DI Number	275	572	1271

60   6

GENERAL INTRODUCTION • INTRODUCTION TO KNOWLEDGE MANAGEMENT • INTRODUCTION TO INNOVATION • INTRODUCTION TO ENTREPRENEURSHIP • INTRODUCTION TO SMES • **CONSTRUCTING KNOWLEDGE VALLEY** • MANAGING FORMAL KNOWLEDGE • USING KVT TO IDENTIFY INNOVATION

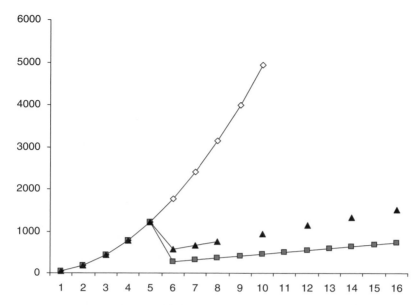

Figure 6.6 **The effect of size of departments on DI in a growing organization.**

'subordinate' in Figure 6.5). In these cases small clusters (i.e. low DI) are linked to a gatekeeper rather than plugging into the DI of the larger super-ordinate department. Although this again indicates the supremely important role of the information gatekeeper (see Chapter 3, sections 3.3 and 3.4), such vertical links will not be considered further here because the topic of this book is DI in (primarily) small enterprises and explaining the rather more complicated mathematics would take too much space for what – for SMEs – would be rare exceptions. However in large organizations the effect is truly punishing. An example is Case 5:

Case 5

The costs of organizational structure

A German specialist chemicals company sold unique chemical reagents to a laboratory in the research division of a multinational pharmaceutical company. Because of the very positive feedback we got from this lab, we tried to get the corporation to put our product in their retail reagents catalogue. However Sales was a different department from Research. So the message went up and up through the Research department, through various gatekeepers, eventually it arrived at sub-board level, crossed over the organization diagram to the correct (Sales) department and began slowly to filter down again to operational levels. This process took two years of hard and frustrating work. When it was completed we found out that the offices of the two people involved (i.e. the relevant two employees from the two divisions involved) were actually situated on the same floor of the same building, working only about 20 meters away from each other!

6.2 The third dimension

The third dimension of the analysis is given by the J-curve, because the J-curve represents a transition where – put simply – things get worse before they get better. Imagine a farmer who saves up for a more powerful combine harvester. While saving, his standard of living (available cash) drops until such time as the purchase can be accomplished, whereupon increased efficiency will drive his standard of living up again, to a level presumably higher than the original level. Many examples of this 'it gets worse before it gets better' effect are known from several disciplines, e.g. medicine.

6.2.1 The hockey stick curve

There are many curves around masquerading as J-curves, and it seems that it is not only fashionable to call a curve after a letter of the alphabet, but also that these can be 'flavour of the month'. An example is the Bass curve, immortalized by Rogers (1983) in his book *The diffusion of innovators*; while actually resembling an 'f', it, and other hysteresis-like curves similar to those described for Chaos theory (see e.g. Williams, 1997) are often incorrectly called 'S' curves.[2]

Having sorted out which curves erroneously resemble letters of the alphabet, let us look more closely at 'J-curves' (Figure 6.7). An early example of the J-curve stems from the work of James Davies (Davies, 1962). He describes the differences, and growth of a gap, between rising expectations and social reality in certain economic situations.

Shortly, in situations that are getting 'better', the pace of reality does not keep up with ambitious expectations. For example, as men walked on the Moon apparently routinely in the early 1970s, most people in the US expected Mars to be colonized by the year 2000 at the latest. Interestingly Davies work from the 1960s is still very relevant because it is often applied today in reorganizing large corporations to be more innovative and efficient, as seen in Figure 6.8.

But as far as we are concerned, Davies J-curve is pointing in the wrong direction, i.e. it is upside down. The J-curve that we shall use is similar the 'hockeystick' curve used to describe investment in a new venture (see e.g. Figure 1.1 in Bygrave & Timmons, 1992). This type of curve, and in this orientation, is widely used for example in economics to describe e.g. devaluation (or depreciation) due to low price elasticity following changes in international exchange rates (i.e. a transient worsening in the national balance of payments due to inelastic demand for imports and exports).

---

[2] A truly 'S'-shaped curve would be bizarre: Imagine time on the X-axis plotted against the severity of the weather on the Y axis. An S curve intersects up to three times, so the weather on one day could be heat-wave, driving rain and freezing blizzard, simultaneously! A meteorological impossibility.

GENERAL INTRODUCTION • INTRODUCTION TO KNOWLEDGE MANAGEMENT • INTRODUCTION TO INNOVATION • INTRODUCTION TO ENTREPRENEURSHIP • INTRODUCTION TO SMES • **CONSTRUCTING KNOWLEDGE VALLEY** • MANAGING FORMAL KNOWLEDGE • USING KVT TO IDENTIFY INNOVATION

62   6

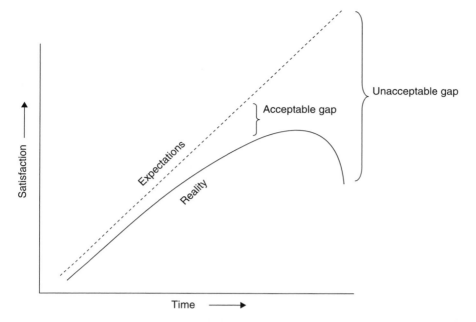

Figure 6.7 **The Davies 'inverted J-curve'. Taken from Davies (1962).**

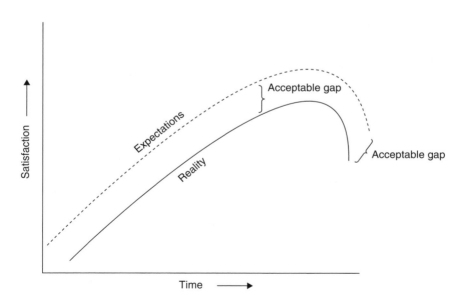

Figure 6.8 **How Business Process Reengineering (BPR) consultants try to manage the acceptance gap by keeping expectations close to reality. Taken from Davies (1962).**

This is the curve described by a swimmer diving into a pool. Imagine the swimmer standing on the right; he has lost his watch, which is lying on the bottom of the pool a few meters away from the edge. The swimmer dives into the water in a shallow dive. During this part of the dive his trajectory is essentially linear. If the watch was lying a long way off, this would not be the case because the swimmer would be slowed by both air and water resistance during the huge leap needed. Similarly if the swimmer started his trajectory on a high diving board, then gravity would impart a significant acceleration on the way down (this is why jumping off a high building is quite safe, only hitting the ground is dangerous). However in our example, the short distances involved mean that all of these factors are negligible. So our swimmer passes the air/water interface and continues on to reach and recover the watch. At this point the swimmer, realizing that the air in his lungs is running out, will switch to a steeper inclination so as to get back to the surface quickly, i.e. the left hand of the curve is steeper than the right-hand side. The shape of the left of the curve can be quite variable depending on various factors like if the curve we draw starts at his eyes or at his feet (so let us assume we have taken his centre of gravity), whether he panics and surfaces quickly, or if he is enjoying himself and 'bottoms out' for an extra stroke and so on. Thus the left-hand curve upwards can range from a rather narrow half-parabola, to a wide sector of a logarithmic spiral. In both cases the curve can easily be described by mathematics: The parabola by using a Cartesian equation[3] or spiral by using Fibonacci numbers. The point is that that later in this book (starting in Chapter 14) we will be taking a generic J-curve, but – just like different companies starting up – the individual hockey stick curves may differ from the generic case. Clearly a new pharmaceutical company will have a different hockey stick curve investment needs from e.g. a new hairdressers salon, but that this does not invalidate the generic curve, because individual cases varying from the generic can always be calculated according to Fibonacci, Cartesian or other equations.

The 'getting worse before it gets better' J-curve is also seen turning existing companies around or other performance-improving exercises. The term 'Business Process Reengineering' (BPR) has fallen somewhat into disfavour, but this and its allied tools (change management etc.) consist to a large extent of managing over-optimistic short-term expectations about company performance (i.e. a Davis J-curve, as seen in Figure 6.8) upon introducing new technology, often including new management techniques. To put it shortly, BPR is not only about buying new hardware, suppressing the inevitable middle-management revolt etc., but convincing the board of directors that their analysis of the short-term

---

[3] The Cartesian equation referred to is: $y = ax^2 + bx + c$.

    Fibonacci numbers, among other things, describe e.g. the growing spiral curvature on snail, ammonite and so on shells where the distances between the turnings of a logarithmic spiral increase in geometrical progression. This is in contrast to the Archimedean spiral, where these distances are constant.

GENERAL INTRODUCTION • INTRODUCTION TO KNOWLEDGE MANAGEMENT • INTRODUCTION TO INNOVATION • INTRODUCTION TO ENTREPRENEURSHIP • INTRODUCTION TO SMES • **CONSTRUCTING**

64   6   **KNOWLEDGE VALLEY** • MANAGING FORMAL KNOWLEDGE • USING KVT TO IDENTIFY INNOVATION

benefits are often over-optimistic and that the long-term benefits are probably understated! For example (Case 6):

Case 6

Getting the timing right

In 1998 many fledgling companies were trying to get on the Internet wave, but their short-term plans were often highly over-optimistic and they crashed (the so-called 'dot com bust' of 2000), however the long-term benefits were also under-estimated and in fact the volume of Internet shopping and trade ten years later in 2008 simply drowned the wildest 1998 fantasy. By 2010 all commerce had become e-commerce.

A different set of barriers emerge when looking at benefits of BPR – it is very hard to quantify in value terms how much has been added. This in turn revolves around two points: how much the organization involved would have increased in value anyway, and the fact that various tools ('Tobins q', 'EVA', 'Balanced Scorecard' and similar approaches like the 'Skandia Navigator' and 'Intangible Asset Monitor') tend to give significantly differing results. One thing is certain, however; a company undergoing BPR or similar process starts at a certain value – perhaps its stock trading price – and the value will very probably decrease before it increases again (i.e. a hockey-stick type J-curve like Figure 6.9).

This is the kind of J-curve recently used by Bremmer (2006) to describe the stability and standard of living of nation-states (on the y-axis) with 'degree of

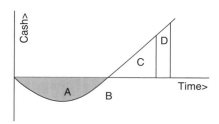

Figure 6.9 **The 'J-Curve' or 'hockey stick curve' for capital demand relating to new investment vehicles. Initial negative cash flow in amounts equal to the area labelled A is gradually offset by sales to reach break-even point (B). Thus A equals total investment needs (normally broken down by quarter, as detailed in the marketing plan). When positive returns are achieved the company eventually reaches a point where investments have been covered, i.e. the area of A is equal to the area of C. This equates to the basic Return on Investment (RoI) time. When further profits are returned – typically when D > 35% of C – then investors are ready to sell to later investors. Modified from Mellor (2003a).**

openness' (on the x-axis). Bremmer used the J-curve not only to illustrate differences in national government, but interestingly, to encourage the concept of manageable change before the country in question breaks apart.

Thus, as we have seen above, the J-curve has been used to plot investments (i.e. value), depreciation (i.e. value), stability (i.e. value) and standard of living (i.e. value) against either time from instantiation or 'openness'. Clearly this openness can also be taken to reflect degree of intellectual interchange and communication, i.e. the very factors we have seen are part and parcel of the 'mutual inspiration' concept central to 'diversity innovation' (see Chapter 3, section 3.2) and indeed to Knowledge Management. However – with the trivial exception of time divisions in some cases – the models developed until now share one enormous disadvantage; they all lack units. Therefore they are not quantifiable.

The 'hockey-stick' J-curve plots investments against time, but these are for individual cases (and opening a pizzeria or hairdresser salon is very different, in investment terms, to developing a new medicine or space ship). Similarly the price elasticity example and the J-curve of Bremmer (2006) are both simply unquantifiable effects, without any kind of units attached. This is similar to our swimmer example, where the bottom of the pool (where the lost watch has come to rest) describes the lowest point, without specifying the depth at that point. But clearly there is a difference (for the swimmer) between a depth of 2 meters and 200 meters! Thus it is essential that we strive to try to attach actual measurable values to the axes.

6.2.2 Putting values on the axis

Bremmer (2006) postulates that nations have to democratize and thus must travel along the J-curve from left to right (like a 'hockey-stick' capital investment curve) in order to emerge higher at the right-hand side, in terms of standard of living. The point of BRP exercises is similar, namely to transit a company along a J-curve from a low point to a higher value at the right-hand side. Clearly in order to achieve or derive any kind of meaningful results using a J-curve, we need to attach values. At this point we can retrieve the original (inverted) J-curve idea as described by James Davies (Davies, 1962) and build on it by using values we know from BPR. When a BPR project starts, the organization involved initially (typically) loses money. This is partly due to physical reorganizations temporarily interrupting production, lower productivity until operators have been retrained, small acts of sabotage by middle managers that can see their jobs disappearing, large payments to BPR consultants like me and so on.

At the low point the value of a commercial company undergoing BPR may be decreased by 40%. This means that an organization worth 10 million will be down to 6 million. This is the practical value seen and reported by BPR professionals, e.g. McKinsey, Accenture, Deloitte and others (including myself, and I did BPR consulting for six years!). Obviously it does not represent the lowest possible value, as there is nothing to stop the company worth 10 million from going down to zero, or even 10 million in the red! It is just that if the value drops below the 40% rule of thumb, then the firm will probably not survive, i.e. the BPR has not had a successful outcome ('the operation was a success but the patient is dead'). Thus we can use BPR to provisionally estimate that the lowest point on the J-curve is 40% lower than the starting point. Similarly we can estimate the difference in height of the starting and finishing points – always subject to the difficulties in measuring value mentioned above. Taking a traditional company as starting point and transforming it, a successful BPR project will, at maturity, approximately triple the value of an organization (noting that exact figures are not possible to e.g. the nature of accounting practices, inflation and that the world will have moved on). Higher values – reaching up to 10 or 15 – have been reported by e.g. Lillrank and Holopainen (1998), but these are regarded in the industry as being very special cases and are much trickier to compare as they often pertain to newer companies i.e. comparing Internet-based companies like Amazon with a purely theoretical non-Internet baseline. In fact the Lillrank and Holopainen (1998) study also specifically included two high scorers – Telia and Nokia.

The above estimates using BPR values, inserted into the Bremmer-type J-curve, would result in a curve that looks reassuringly correct (as we would expect since the process is comparable to those in the 'hockey-stick' capital investment curve), but we really need some kind of supporting data before we can sign it off.

To do this, we can look at other organization types. Interestingly, the original Bremmer (2006) J-curve postulates that the y-axis represents not only national stability (obviously without units) but also reflects citizens' standard of living. We can compare J-curves for commercial companies with those for nation-states, providing that we are clear that some differences exist. The most obvious example is that commercial companies operate within relatively narrow economic bands due to cash-flow restraints which nations rarely have. Conversely nations – not enterprises – may be subject to sanctions by other nations and indeed may still exist as nation-states even when ruinously bankrupt.

Unfortunately, Bremmer was too cautious to venture much more into the direction of putting actual values on the y-axis of his J-curve, but one can in fact easily find figures which reflect the average standard of living, e.g. Gross Domestic Product, for all nation-states, including those Bremmer mentions. Some of these are given in Table 6.2 in approximate ascending order of 'political stability and openness' and indeed one can see that these data points would lie on a J-curve (see Figure 6.10).

Despite the fact that the dots representing various selected nation-states at various stability points seem to fit the J-curve, the sceptic may well raise various objections e.g. 'Afghanistan is a special case', 'what about Equatorial Guinea with a per capita GDP of $50,200?', 'ten points don't make a curve' and so on. All of these objections (and several more) are quite true and valid. However there

Table 6.2 **GDP per capita for selected nation-states, illustrating the Bremmer (2006) J-curve. Data taken from the CIA World Fact Book 2008.**

Nation state	GDP per capita ($)
North Korea	1700
Bhutan	1400
Afghanistan	800
Yemen	900
Zambia	900
China	6800
Russia	11,000
Poland	13,100
United Kingdom	30,100
United States	41,600

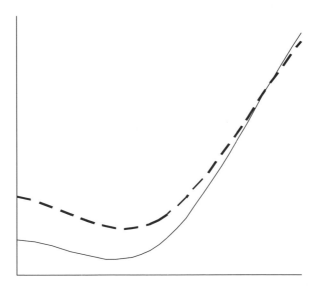

Figure 6.10 **The J-curve taking either GDP per capita (unbroken line) across a spectrum of national openness, or annual profit per employee throughout a typical BPR project (dashed line). Note that the curves have been subjected to a mathematical smoothing algorithm.**

will always be special cases and approximations are all that we can achieve, the major point is that Figure 6.10 shows that the general shape of the curve corresponds quite well independently of whether we use BPR data, or geopolitical data and this is the important point since the shape of the curve between the extremities is determined by Cartesian or other mathematics. However there are discrepancies.

68 6

GENERAL INTRODUCTION • INTRODUCTION TO KNOWLEDGE MANAGEMENT • INTRODUCTION TO INNOVATION • INTRODUCTION TO ENTREPRENEURSHIP • INTRODUCTION TO SMES • **CONSTRUCTING KNOWLEDGE VALLEY** • MANAGING FORMAL KNOWLEDGE • USING KVT TO IDENTIFY INNOVATION

The major discrepancy is that in the geopolitical data the extreme y-value is some 20 times that of the extreme left value and this is a larger multiple than the BPR data would indicate, where 10 would be regarded as exceptionally high. A further minor point is that the BPR data starts at baseline and dips by up to 40%, the geopolitical data also dips around 50% from the starting values but in the geopolitical data the left-hand extreme starts already well below the baseline (world average GDP = $9500 pc). The reason for this difference is however quite simple – that bankrupt states can keep going, but bankrupt companies (in a Capitalist democracy) cannot!

However it is reassuring that the two comparisons (derived from figures based both BPR on organizations and from the GDP of nation-states) do seem to allow us to attach financial value to the axis; this was previously purely intuitive and although there is nothing wrong with intuition, things like the divorce statistics would seem to impress upon us the importance of some kind of independent verification – even if it is an approximation – is prudent. So here we have our instinct, plus two verifications taken from wildly different situations, and this could persuade most people to mumble the 'yes' word – despite the risks!

An extra word of explanation is due here; the values estimated and used in Figure 6.10 for commercial companies are for SMEs. But SMEs are only part (but a large part) of the national economy. Since larger companies achieve this kind of performance and more, plus pay dividends, tax and so on, then it may be that for them, both ends of the J-curve are steeper and higher, but this question exceeds the topic of this book.

Having established some key values on the y-axis, the units on the x-axis can be established. At first this looks unlikely, because just like there are no units for national stability; there are simply no units for innovation (neither 'microinnos' nor 'innos', nor 'kiloinnos' etc.). However what we can use instead is a 1–100 scale where the value is the amount derived from the maximum (100%) possible. We can do this because the maximum possible, for an organization of known size (number of employees) can always be calculated from Equation 6.1.

6.2.3   Adding topology

The 3D curve consists of growth (measured as number of employees) on the x-axis, relative innovation (as % of maximum) on the y-axis and either annual turnover or annual profitability per employee (i.e. in money terms) on the z-axis. The DI net is the weft and weave of the landscape of the 3D fold, or valley, which we are about to create.

In order to provide 3D curve we have to use our fantasy a little because we want first to establish the borders of the curve (although it is actually a 3D fold), i.e. we have to go to the extremes while still remaining realistic. We saw in Figure 6.6 and Table 6.1 that the way to maximize DI in a growing organization is to allow the number of employees (P) to grow to almost-unmanageable numbers (around 50) then split the organization into two similar (in terms of numbers of employees) departments. The figure of 50, despite being ignored by conventional SME wisdom, is one which recurs often (e.g. '... If we had 1000 people I would like to think of them as being 20 teams of 50...' a successful SME owner cited by Mazzarol, 2003). Clearly the next step is, as each of these departments grows again to 50, split each of them again down the middle, making 4 departments of 25, which can grow again to 4 departments of 50 before the next fission takes place (Figure 6.11). Those of you with a biological tendency will find this model peculiarly reminiscent of bacterial cell division or a growing foetus. In forming the foetus two unequal cells meet (i.e. DI = 1) and fuse. The resulting fertilized cell (the zygote) swells and splits into two equally sized cells. These two similar cells grow until both divide (almost simultaneously) to form a cluster of 4 cells, which grow until another fission gives rise to 8 cells, and so forth, at least until the blastomere (about 24 cell) stage is reached. Thus there may be vague parallels in the development of organisms and the development of organizations (several authors, e.g. Ormerod (2005), have previously made such claims[4]).

So if we now revisit Equation 6.1, the formula DI =P*[P-1]/2 can easily be converted into scripting code like:

For   (P=1; P<51; DI = P*[P−1]/2; P++)

Equation 6.4: Code for generating a curve showing the amount of diversity innovation in a population between 1 and 50 persons.

Thus, using derivations of Equations 6.2 and 6.4, we can convert the simple fission model (Figure 6.11) into a curve too:

For   (P=1; P<51; DI = P*[P−1]/2; P++)
For   (P=51; P<101; D=2; DI=[P*(P−1)]/4*D+[D*(D−1)/2; P++)
For   (P=101; P<201; D=4; DI=[P*(P−1)]/8*D+[D*(D−1)/2; P++)

Figure 6.11 **The simple fission model used to determine maximum DI. When the organization grows to 50 employees, it splits into two equally sized parts, each of which grow until they, in turn, reach 50 persons each, whereupon they grow equally until they reach size 50 and so on**

---

[4] In his book 'Why things fail' Ormerod (2005) makes the fine point that individuals (psychologically), species (biologically) and organizations (economically) are seldom – in fact almost never – absolute maximizers. Although Ormerod falls down a little on his biology, e.g. in confusing ecology with evolution, this does not detract much from the probable overall validity of his thesis.

GENERAL INTRODUCTION · INTRODUCTION TO KNOWLEDGE MANAGEMENT · INTRODUCTION TO INNOVATION · INTRODUCTION TO ENTREPRENEURSHIP · INTRODUCTION TO SMES · **CONSTRUCTING**

70   6   **KNOWLEDGE VALLEY** · MANAGING FORMAL KNOWLEDGE · USING KVT TO IDENTIFY INNOVATION

Equation 6.5: A scripting model for generating a curve showing the amount of diversity innovation in a population between 1 and 200 persons, splitting the organizations into equally sized parts when they reach size 50. This code is written here in a generic fashion, but may be written in code for mathematical applications e.g. MATLAB or other commonly used languages; in fact in this work Maple11 was used.

This can now be used to generate a curve.

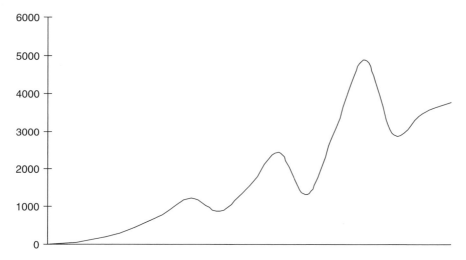

Figure 6.12 **Diversity innovation number in a population between 1 and 250 (i.e. the top limit for SME classification) employees, splitting the organizations into equally sized parts when they reach size 50. Note that the curve has been subjected to an additional mathematical smoothing algorithm (in MS Excel).**

The curve above (Figure 6.12) was generated using Equation 6.5 and increments of 20, plus an additional smoothing function which is allowable because in a growing situation involving fission and forming new departments – like in Figure 6.11 – not all connections will be severed instantaneously, i.e. upon reorganizing one large department into two smaller departments, mutual contact between separated individuals will be retained for some time, although this will fade, as well as being diluted by new arrivals and staff turnover.

A word of caution here, the curve in Figure 6.12 is the DI number, representing the number of ties in an organization or the numbers of ways individuals employed there can communicate – it is not a representation of the total 'stockpile' of knowledge in an organization!

Clearly the above curve is 'frilly'. The troughs can theoretically be ameliorated by dividing the workforce unequally, e.g. DI for 60 persons (although this can hardly be achieved) is 1770 and dividing the workforce into 2 departments of 30 will reduce DI, whereas retaining 50 in 1 department and siphoning 10 off into a new department results in a significantly higher DI (see Table 6.1). Thus uneven splitting into two differently sized departments may be more stable, depending on the situation and this may be especially relevant or attractive when e.g. starting a new site, opening an office abroad, a change in the market and so on.

The other extreme will be to minimize DI. The value which is mathematically most satisfying is to keep DI = 0 as the organization grows. In Figure 6.12 this simply represents the X-axis (i.e. Figure 6.12 actually represents the 'floor' of the 3D fold). In the z-dimension of the 3D figure this is done by simply incrementing turnover for every new employee, but postulating that they rarely interact with each other. It is rather hard to see how such an unnatural situation can arise in real life, but remember that although we are sticking to zero, the x-axis on the curve is relative innovation, so zero really means the relative minimum; the least possibly achievable, even if this implies a chilling Dickensian or Tayloristic environment (some people may prefer 'Newtonian' as the opposite of innovative or 'Schumpeterian', but in fact many mechanistic – 'Newtonian' – companies do very well and clockwork-type management mechanisms may be highly appropriate to certain branches of industry e.g. the production of sugar, flour, nails and other basic goods). The resulting 3D fold is formed of the 2D Figure 6.12 and the third dimension consists of the BPR curve of profitability per employee as shown in Figure 6.10.

The most chilling observation upon observing this fold is that the second round of departmentalization – the transition from 'small' to 'medium-sized' at an organizational size of around 90,110 employees cuts the DI number (and profitability?) down to the very bottom of the J-curve. In the Grainer model of SME development (see Chapter 5, section 5.3) it may correspond to the end of stage 2 – the 'Crisis of autonomy'. This underlines the importance of owners getting this step right. Typically in SMEs during the first departmentalization round, partners and old friends are often brought in as department leaders for reasons

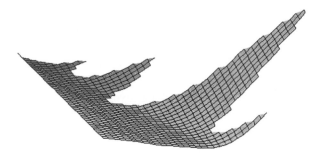

Figure 6.13 **The basic topography of the knowledge valley for organizations of size up to 250 employees in terms of estimated productivity per employee (see Table 14.1 for the values used).**

of trust and familiarity. However Figure 6.13 shows that this strategy cannot reasonably be continued – or at least not with high chances of success – during the second round of departmentalization. Figure 6.13 shows that splitting the company into four equal sized departments brings the DI number down dramatically and the organization slips down the J-curve into negative values. It must be underlined that these are real values as measured by money-equivalents (value per person per year). Thus the second round of departmentalization should be when 'real' leaders who are professionals, capable managers and good information gatekeepers (see Chapter 3, section 3.5) need to be put in place.

The curve in Figure 6.13 can now be added in order to create a better map of the valley: up to now the J-curve has been represented as value per person per year, so multiplying by the number of people (which we can read off from the X-axis), and calculating that employees in a gazelle will be higher paid on average, we can see the size of a given corporation in estimated annual turnover. See Table 14.1 for the actual conversion values used here. This new scale has the advantage of being the measure with which most people in the field are better acquainted with. At the same time the perspective (Figure 6.14 is viewed from the right-hand side of Figure 6.13) can be reversed so that the valley can better be seen.

Figure 6.14 **The derived topology of the knowledge valley for organizations of size up to 250 employees in terms of estimated annual turnover for the organizations (see Table 14.1 for values of the Z axis).**

6.2.4 Populating the knowledge ecosphere

Companies inhabit the Knowledge Valley and, as shown in Table 5.3, there are various classifications of SMEs. In biology, species can evolve, but not individuals. A particular animal (if it is not a giraffe) cannot in its lifetime become a giraffe no matter how much it stretches its neck. Translated into a business universe;

existing large firms are seldom capable of using innovation, e.g. of the Fortune 100 companies from 1930, only one (General Electric) still exists.

In the business universe it is branches of industry – the business world's equivalent to species – that evolve. But in business, in contrast to biology, individual companies can also occasionally evolve into something else: e.g. the Preussische Bergwerks und Hutten Aktiengesellschaft (Prussian Society for Mining and Smelting) became tourist giant TUI and the Nokianvirta Paper Mill became the mobile telephony giant Nokia. Similarly, in the SME business world, an individual mouse can, if it wants to and if environmental conditions are right, successfully evolve into another animal, namely gazelles or elephants. In this section we will be placing gazelles, elephants and mice in the knowledge valley according to the following criteria: a mouse is per definition at or near the origin, which corresponds well with its precarious capital position just above the lapping waters of the tarn. Gazelles, as high-value beasts, will be at the right-hand side of the curve shown in Figure 6.15, a position probably corresponding well to where one could instinctively put them on the curve represented in Figure 6.12. It may be unfair to place elephants on the left side of the curve shown in Figure 6.10, as this should be reserved for the most Dickensian of sweat-shops, however one must consider the 'bleak house' scenario of employment in SMEs (e.g. Ram, 1994) supported by

Figure 6.15 **The geography of knowledge valley for organizations of size up to 200 employees and using annual turnover for the organizations (see Table 14.1 for values of the Z axis) and showing the tarn and the positions of the various categories of SME – mouse, gazelles and elephants.**

statistics from work tribunals and generally exposing widespread poor employee relations in many SMEs.[5]

To be more optimistic however, one should consider that elephants inhabit a zone around the higher reaches of the tarn, and may well exist on the gazelle side of the valley bottom.

6.2.5   Knowledge trails in the valley

For the purposes of this model we will assume that an SME is 'born' as a new start-up. This micro-organization may consist of one person, so the DI is 0 and in fact, in the moment of new venture creation, the turnover is very close to zero. Thus the tiny 'mouse' occupies the origin of the graph. In principle, one would now wish to tip-toe around any innovation chasms (Figure 3.5) and trail-blaze the watershed up to the 'Peaks of Performance'. In practice however, few would try to conquer the rocky peaks and instead more well trodden 'knowledge trails' will come into existence along the valley. Most companies are reluctant learners, happy to exist, to be making a profit, going for moderately safe goals and unwilling to disturb the balance by introducing risky changes. This can be represented in simple terms as a 'preferred relationships' in the DI node net of ties which forms the weft and weave of the valley structure (Figure 6.16):

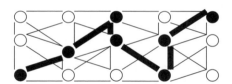

Figure 6.16 **Illustrating a knowledge trail of preferred relationships through a simplified DI network.**

SME owners trek across the Knowledge Valley in directions affected both by their (conscious or not) choice and by the 'weather' of the Porterian Forces (see Porter, 1980) bearing down on them. For some, the Porterian weather will be mild and sunny, for others gale and sleet. Thus the knowledge trails formed will differ from owner to owner, depending on whim, branch and circumstances. Circumstances may sometimes be transient (e.g. boom) or fixed (e.g. location). Some owners will hang up their walking boots at a convenient perch and enjoy the

---

[5] In the 1970s, smaller companies were held up as being viable alternatives to larger companies, but the 'happy ship' scenario developed by Ingham (1979) and others has since been questioned by academics whose research included not only the managers, but also the managed (e.g. Ram, 1994). This led to the 'bleak house' scenario, supported by statistics from work tribunals and generally exposing widespread poor employer–employee relations in small companies.

view; others may force a way up their path for some distance, but decide not to join with a summit party. These strategies are referred to as 'capped growth' or similar (for a convenient review, see McMahon, 1998) and may simply reflect that the owners lifestyle is satisfied, or a reluctance on part of the owner to take on external investors to finance further growth, or other factors. However, as seen before, owners can get a boost by e.g. manipulating department size (see e.g. Table 6.1) which may be beneficial if the company in question is already on the gazelle side of the Tarn, but those on the left-hand Taylor side may find that by boosting DI they slip down the J-curve into the murky waters of the Tarn of Knowledge Valley (see Figure 6.14 and the Chapter 7), so relaxing the iron grip of Dickensian conditions may paradoxically leave the company floundering and reduced in value!

Case 7

Organizational structure and performance are interdependent

Certainly I observed in one Scottish organization, which shall remain anonymous, that a strong and autocratic leader actually and deliberately surrounded himself with weak personalities in middle management positions. Probably that person did not plan on leaving, but situations often change and he did leave. This meant that uncertainty ensued and outputs plummeted as soon as the leader and his iron grip were no longer present, and his 'yes-men' were too weak to fill the gap. That organization never properly recovered.

Leaders know that management vacuums need to be filled, but few can do it well.

6.2.6 Public sector: The tarn of knowledge valley

The surface of the Tarn of Knowledge Valley in the middle of the J-curve (thus in the centre of the valley) is taken as being −5% because this is an approximate limit as to how much loss a company can take over a prolonged period of time, although it must be freely admitted that the value of −5% could just as easily be another value. The exact value will be rather hazy, as the Tarn will also have 'tides', i.e. move up and down the beach according to external influences. Just as solar and lunar movements influence the height of a real body of water; the Tarn of Knowledge Valley will experience ebb and flow due to changing bank interest rates, inflation, the availability of credit, exchange rates and so on.

Many researchers in the Small Business field claim to look at 'all' organizations (e.g. Stokes, 2002) but actually only include commercial ones. But in fact the loss-making depths of the Tarn of Knowledge Valley also contain 'living' organisms, the most obvious of which are giant squids; ministries and other government organizations that make huge annual losses (i.e. the opposite of immediate commercial profit) at bathypelagic depths which exceed the employee limit of this model. At our – more moderate – epipelagic depth, these are more akin to bivalve molluscs and crabs, which represent the smaller state bureaux and similar organizations. These are truly at the lowest depths of the J-curve because the pull up to the right of the J-curve; towards efficiency and better public service (including modernization and innovative e-government initiatives, etc.) is equally balanced by a pull to autocracy and the left of the J-curve (political expedients, the dominance of political targets, civil service 'empire-building', etc.), leaving them always around the lowest point. The Product Life Cycle (Kotler & Armstrong, 1989) analogy is often applied co-commercial enterprises and if the same can be applied to such organizations, then surely these are the zombies,* simply unable to die due to constant infusions of public money!

In Chapter 6, section 6.1.4 I argue that an organization should adopt a rounded form because; 'threats and opportunities can come without warning from any angle, thus a 'well rounded', flowing or even amoeboid structure is that which will survive best over more rigid forms'. Smaller (i.e. up to 249 employees) state bureaux and similar organizations (QUANGOs, NGOs etc.) are often very 'sharp' i.e. they exist for a specific purpose. This means that express policies around Knowledge Management are rare, and plans involving Information Systems strategy are often make-do while public profile and specific political objectives – the low hanging fruit – are high on the organizational priority list. Success in Information Systems projects is based on the organizational plan for several years ahead. A general election or other political scandal changes a governmental organization's overall mission, including in terms of objectives and milestones that govern the mission as well as the steps needed to reach these goals. Thus a change of political 'leadership' will render an application portfolio/IT architecture defunct overnight. The situation is exacerbated by the lack of cost/benefit thinking at political (i.e. taxpayer-funded) level. One four-year project was well on track and fulfilling expectations when a general election changed government and the lead player (myself) was called in to explain why progress did not meet the new expectations. My initial response was 'lack of appreciation of IT and indeed any computer literacy – bordering on the imbecility – at the political level'. Needless to say I moderated my remarks.

Some considerations of larger public organizations are considered in Chapter 14. Many of these have a truly spectacular failure record, one case in point being the deservedly well-criticized Child Support Agency, a branch of the UK Department of Work and Pensions.

6.2.7 Social entrepreneurship: The beach of knowledge valley

However in reality the picture of life around the Tarn is much more differentiated than the black-and-white picture I have painted above: In fact the beaches and rock pools of the littoral zone around the tarn are also teeming with life; charities, non-profit and not-for-profit organizations abound. All these exist around zero on the profitability axis – but they are far from dead! The spectrum of ethical/social activity stretches from not-for-profit organizations, through dedicated ethical non-profit models, and finally ending in outright charities working in an absolutely non-commercial (i.e. perpetual loss-making, seen from a strictly accounting point of view) environment, and these in turn are often reliant on voluntary unpaid workers. This basis of voluntary work – sense of mission – and the very lack of employer–employee relations promote knowledge sharing and new innovative models leading to success (whatever 'success' may be for that organization).

Social and religious voluntary organizations have a strong history of being major providers in both the health and education sectors (see e.g. Bifulco in Mellor, 2008), indeed the Peter F. Drucker Foundation (www.pfdf.org) reckons that the combined value of social entrepreneurship outweighs that of commercial entrepreneurship. The beach of the tarn is the active biosphere of social entrepreneurship.

78　6

GENERAL INTRODUCTION · INTRODUCTION TO KNOWLEDGE MANAGEMENT · INTRODUCTION TO INNOVATION · INTRODUCTION TO ENTREPRENEURSHIP · INTRODUCTION TO SMES · **CONSTRUCTING KNOWLEDGE VALLEY** · MANAGING FORMAL KNOWLEDGE · USING KVT TO IDENTIFY INNOVATION

GENERAL   INTRODUCTION   •   INTRODUCTION   TO   KNOWLEDGE   MANAGEMENT   •
CTION TO INNOVATION • INTRODUCTION TO ENTREPRENEURSHIP • INTRODUCTION
• CONSTRUCTING KNOWLEDGE VALLEY • MANAGING FORMAL KNOWLEDGE • USING
KVT TO IDENTIFY INNOVATION BOOSTING FACTORS • FACTORS THAT STOP INNOVATION
• A SUMMARY OF LESSONS LEARNT FROM KVT • RECOMBINING KNOWLEDGE AND
LEARNING PROVOKES INSPIRATION • SOME CONCLUSIONS AND SUMMING UP • CHOOSING
POSSIBLE TECHNOLOGIES • CALCULATE YOUR BENEFIT • LARGER ORGANIZATIONS

7 managing formal knowledge

Although managing formal knowledge, in the sense of managing a portfolio of patents, is well beyond the scope of this book, some aspects do merge quite well and are worth mentioning here.

Here we will not be dealing with process or concept issues around IP, but considerations are restricted to the place of formal IP in the abstract concept called Knowledge Valley Theory.

Some start-ups (by definition 'mice') with formal and protected knowledge, often a patent or patent application, rightly or wrongly assume that they will end up as gazelles. To some extent this can be facilitated by the natural structure or field of activity of the organization. For example, in a biotechnology start-up the considerable overlap between proteomics and genomics will imply that departmentalization – or at least division based on the technical specialities of the workforce – will not be drastic and that the DI number will not show such violent troughs as are apparent in Figures 6.12 and 6.13, i.e. the watershed is more regular. Nonetheless, because formal IP, once published and thus externalized (see Chapter 2, section 2.1), is become largely independent of DI. Such patents can therefore be thought of as being outside the DI net and forming slender rope bridges between peaks. The innovation stemming from an earlier period in the evolution of that organization is not lost and can bridge troughs to be of use to the organization at a later time.

These bridges are, however, extremely delicate. Indeed one never knows the true value of a patent until it is either sold (in licence or other form) or challenged in open court, by which time it is often too late.

The difficulties include:

- Lack of flexibility: for too many small firms 1 patent = 1 product = 1 start-up. Thus environmental changes ('earth tremors' in our geological valley analogy) will bring the whole structure tumbling down.
- The cost of maintaining a patent will often exhaust a small company; certainly the costs of seriously defending a single patent will drive most small or medium-sized organizations to the verge of bankruptcy and over.

Indeed engineering a robust solution is difficult. The most adopted approach is to shore up the delicate 1-patent bridge with more IPR buttresses and girders. In practice these are secondary patents (i.e. if the original patent is on a substance, then secondary patents can be on the processes involved in making it or packaging it). Other rights or protection mechanisms like trademarks, or trade secrets, can help stabilize the structure and defend it against adverse influence. Obviously selling many licences also helps 'root' the structure, as courts will be unlikely to overthrow patent rights that have been widely licensed.

Clearly there is much more that can be said on managing IP and Intellectual Property Rights, e.g. due diligence, licensing etc, but these fall well outside the scope of this book. Interested readers are referred to e.g. the book *Patents for Business* by Heines (Heines, 2007) for further details or read the older but clearly and wittily written work by Poltorak and Lerner (2004).

GENERAL INTRODUCTION • INTRODUCTION TO KNOWLEDGE MANAGEMENT • INTRODUCTION TO INNOVATION • INTRODUCTION TO ENTREPRENEURSHIP • INTRODUCTION TO SMES • CONSTRUCTING KNOWLEDGE VALLEY • **MANAGING FORMAL KNOWLEDGE** • USING KVT TO IDENTIFY INNOVATION

80   7

GENERAL   INTRODUCTION   •   INTRODUCTION   TO   KNOWLEDGE   MANAGEMENT   •
O INNOVATION • INTRODUCTION TO ENTREPRENEURSHIP • INTRODUCTION
RUCTING KNOWLEDGE VALLEY • MANAGING FORMAL KNOWLEDGE • USING
KVT TO IDENTIFY INNOVATION BOOSTING FACTORS • FACTORS THAT STOP INNOVATION
• A SUMMARY OF LESSONS LEARNT FROM KVT • RECOMBINING KNOWLEDGE AND
LEARNING PROVOKES INSPIRATION • SOME CONCLUSIONS AND SUMMING UP • CHOOSING
POSSIBLE   TECHNOLOGIES   •   CALCULATE   YOUR   BENEFIT   •   LARGER   ORGANIZATIONS

Part III   applying theoretical principles

Context and aims

In the previous part of this book we established a theoretical framework upon which to build. Theory is very nice, but all theories have to be tested by asking deep questions that are basically designed to disprove or modify them (e.g. in 1021 Al Hazan showed light travels in straight lines but a millennium later, in 1911, Einstein postulated that light rays can be bent by e.g. gravity and this was confirmed in 1922 by observations of stars passing behind the sun during a total eclipse). However to be quite straightforward, a theory is no good if it cannot deliver practical results.

In the following sections the theory outlined (KVT) is used to investigate some common and everyday – some may say 'natural' – phenomena. As such we hold abstract and mathematical theory up to reality.

At the end of this chapter the reader should be able to competently account for the strategic theories governing the construction of Knowledge Management Systems in organizations.

GENERAL INTRODUCTION • INTRODUCTION TO KNOWLEDGE MANAGEMENT •
CTION TO INNOVATION INTRODUCTION TO ENTREPRENEURSHIP • INTRODUCTION
• CONSTRUCTING KNOWLEDGE VALLEY • MANAGING FORMAL KNOWLEDGE • USING
KVT TO IDENTIFY INNOVATION BOOSTING FACTORS • FACTORS THAT STOP INNOVATION
• A SUMMARY OF LESSONS LEARNT FROM KVT. • RECOMBINING KNOWLEDGE AND
LEARNING PROVOKES INSPIRATION. • SOME CONCLUSIONS AND SUMMING UP • CHOOSING
POSSIBLE TECHNOLOGIES • CALCULATE YOUR BENEFIT • LARGER ORGANIZATIONS

8 using KVT to identify innovation boosting factors

Although the theory of a virtual 'Knowledge Valley' seems to help explain the evolution of SMEs, real value can only be gained if it, to at least some extent, is predictive. Recommendations can also be drawn – SME owners are forced into certain behaviours by Porters Forces, but this is seldom of blizzard of whiteout proportions and owners can, to some extent, steer their own directions. That said, one must assume some kind of target-related rationality on the part of owners and/or managers. Those with experience of business consulting in SME environments will admit that this is a dangerous assumption and may well be at variance with reality when considering that many SME owner/directors behave in rather eccentric ways (to say the least; 'irrational' or 'downright suicidal stupidity' and similar expressions are often heard from professionals in this field).

The following sections are experimental in nature and, whereas the models presented up to now have been generated with a PC, the processing power needed to generate these later curves (presented below) significantly exceeds that which a PC has to offer. Consequently they have been developed using a computer grid (sometimes referred to as a 'cluster'). What these computer-generated situations involve is equivalent to bowling a ball down knowledge valley and mapping where it hits the end (the right-hand side of the curve represented in Figure 6.12, i.e. where it hits on the Figure 6.10 hockey-stick curve), with the exception that the model used here now only extends to 200 employees (in contrast to Figure 6.12, which extends to 250 employees), this is because companies, like organisms, obey Haldane's Principle (Haldane, 1985) of increasing complexity with size. Indeed, using 250 would not increase the resolution of the resulting 'picture', but would marginally exceed the processing power available. What the computer model does is bowl 100 balls randomly down the valley along connections between nodes while distorting the DI net (the fabric of the valley) according to selected variables (which can be programmed into the equation) and plot the result so that trends can be discerned. Since all nodes are directly connected to each other, they are always 'nearest neighbour' and thus balls may well run round in circles. Therefore to save time on these large calculations, a line of code had to be added which stops the balls going backwards (to be more precise, they were prevented from taking paths which would take them to nodes lying between 90° and 240° from the imaginary true line forward). Although this can be criticized as a deterministic choice (see Chapter 10 for a continuation on the theme of choices), this is seen as justified because:

1. Balls infinitely circling within the organization are subject to 'friction' (transaction costs) and may, in real life, simply die out, exhausted.
2. The point was to see the effect on the 'bottom line', i.e. intersecting with the J-curve, using a large but still finite amount of computer power.

The experimental run ends when the last ball reaches the right-hand side of the valley – their exit points showing up as a scatter plot on the J-curve (Figure 6.10). Due to similarities between this technique and rolling a ball around a roulette table, such methods are often called 'Monte Carlo Methods', and the interested reader will be able to look up a theoretical background to these well-established methods without the slightest difficulty. Because the balls (called 'Monte Carlo' balls) are rolled randomly, exact replications will hardly reproduce the exact results shown here, but, by using sufficient (in this case, 100) of them, the trends seen and presented here will be reproducible.

The first two topics represent scenarios which most SMEs can be confronted with and wish to know how to strategically handle, the third is for larger organizations (but still SMEs) and applies the KVT to the various forms of task forces, a transient form of organization known to focus diverse resources from various parts of an organization on a specific problem to quickly reach an innovative solution.

8.1 Multi-specialisms among employees

In a lone and early work Iansiti (1993) refers to individuals able to sustain meaningful and synergistic relationships with others as possessing 'T-shaped skills', referring to depth in a particular discipline but combined with a breadth of understanding of other disciplines. The role of multi-specialists in particular, has recently re-surfaced and has been the subject of much debate: Katz (2004) says, 'research studies … indicate that the broader the range of skills and abilities … the more likely it is that that person will … become a more effective and successful contributing member of the organisation …' and there is increasing evidence connecting multi-skilling and increased innovation: it is believed that multi-specialists, e.g. an engineer with an MBA, or a chemist with a degree in IT, are responsible for around 40 times more innovations (mostly incremental innovations), than people with a single specialization (Mellor, 2005a). These individuals may furthermore be lifelong learners, or those in a second career.

Clearly workplace innovation (in the sense of diversity innovation, see Figure 3.1) is promoted by variety among work disciplines. This could be e.g. the meeting between different people where they are specialists in different fields. The problem with such meetings is that the two (or more) types of expert often have difficulty in understanding each other to the depth needed (recall the case study presented in Chapter 6, section 6.1.2). Therefore workplace innovation (or mutual inspiration, or whatever one wishes to call it) is at its most simple – and powerful – when communication problems do not exist, i.e. where the two or more specialists are literally embodied within the same person. Thus one person – one human brain – is able to look at a problem with the eyes of (say) a geologist and a businessperson, or teacher, simultaneously.

As we saw in Chapter 6, sections 6.1.2 and 6.1.3, it is the transaction costs for communication that is the main barrier hindering this type of innovation because they can be very high, but multi-specialists represent a situation where the transaction costs for this type of cross-discipline communication are zero. In terms of nodes this can be represented as follows:

Figure 8.1 **A representation of a multi-skilled person where the cost of traversing from one node (skill set) to another is removed.**

The above innovation-enhancing effect is especially pronounced where the multi-specialist possesses 'hard' skills and also qualifications in 'soft' subjects. The interface between e.g. R&D and marketing is a typical problem area where participants cannot understand each other. In SMEs this could be e.g. Internet, where misunderstandings between people in the sales force and in the IT department are both common and crucial. Clearly a multi-skilled person straddling this gap is especially innovative and useful. Highly qualified multi-skilled trans-migrants (including returning ex-pats) are an especially notable group (Mellor, 2005a, 2005b), but – to state the obvious – blindly hiring such individuals is not a guaranteed recipe for success and the SME owner or HR department still has to be critical.

So knowledge trails formed by the multi-skilled in this manner will result in up-swellings – drumlins[1] of higher innovation and value – in the knowledge valley. But what conditions are needed to create them and how significant is their placing in the geography in the valley?

In order to see the effect multi-specialists may have, the Monte Carlo computer simulation was run first with a random scattering of ball through such

---

[1] OK I know that in real life drumlins are formed on the valley floor only, but I'm trying to hang on to the geological analogy.

overlapping nodes (multi-specialists) scattered randomly around an organization, a flat DI net (i.e. a net as in Figure 6.12, cut off at 200 on the x-axis and, so to speak, laid out flat). The effect was negligible because of the randomness – since our Monte Carlo balls could randomly take any path and were not captured into any particular knowledge trail (Figure 6.16), improvements at one point were cancelled out at other points.

Thus to see what factors determined the formation of a knowledge trail, overlapping nodes were added to the flat DI net in a linear fashion (i.e. forming a knowledge trail), so the impact points of the Monte Carlo balls bowled down the net from the origin would be likely to cluster together on the right-hand side. If this were a clear trail, one would expect the Monte Carlo balls to impact points on the right-hand side and there to form a scatter plot exhibiting the characteristics of a Probability Density Function (i.e. a Normal, 'Bell' or Gauss curve), however the curves obtained from repeating the process several times showed a platykurtic curve (i.e. where the peak of the distribution is far too low). Thus another variable, the density of overlapping nodes down the knowledge trail, was adjusted until scatter plots with a Normal density[2] with $\mu = 1$ (i.e. the location parameter was centred on the intersection of the knowledge trail with the flattened J-curve) and a scale parameter (σ) of minimum 1.5 were achieved. This more realistic cumulative distribution function was first obtained when the ratio of overlapping nodes to non-overlapping nodes was 1:1, i.e. every second person in the knowledge trail was multi-skilled. This was the case (i.e. the difference in σ was hardly statistically significant) if the overlapping nodes were distributed randomly along the knowledge trail or if deliberately placed in every second position:

Figure 8.2 **The distribution of overlapping nodes (representing the multi-skilled) needed to spontaneously form a working knowledge trail.**

Having determined the conditions needed to spontaneously (as opposed to deliberately, see Figure 6.16) form a knowledge trail we can roll the DI net up into the knowledge valley profile again – that is the right-hand side will no longer be flat, but will be a J-curve as in Figure 6.10. This means that the Monte Carlo ball impact Gauss curves formed due to the knowledge trail will be distorted

---

[2] The meanings of μ and σ can be gathered from any standard textbook on probability and/or statistics. The standard parameters of a Normal density curve are $\mu = 0$ and $\sigma = 1$. Changing μ shifts the curve to the left or right without changing its shape while changing σ makes the shape higher or flatter. A lower value of σ makes the curve higher, whereas a higher value makes it flatter. In the experimental set up described here, σ will rarely attain unity, even when overlapping nodes are placed continuously along a path, so a threshold value of 1.5 was taken, although this choice was admittedly arbitrary.

GENERAL INTRODUCTION · INTRODUCTION TO KNOWLEDGE MANAGEMENT · INTRODUCTION TO INNOVATION · INTRODUCTION TO ENTREPRENEURSHIP · INTRODUCTION TO SMES · CONSTRUCTING KNOWLEDGE VALLEY · MANAGING FORMAL KNOWLEDGE · **USING KVT TO IDENTIFY INNOVATION**

86   8

because – apart from the deepest part of Tarn of Knowledge Valley where the J-curve is flat – the baseline will itself be curved.

As a jumping-off point let us assume we can manufacture spontaneous knowledge trails on both sides of the Tarn. This seems plausible as the multi-skilled that we will introduce into the organizations will presumably be middle management, i.e. not unskilled nor super top management, so we can use their presumed salary level to identify a band of value above the tarn shoreline. On the left-hand side of the tarn – the elephant shore rising to the Dickensian extreme – the land slopes up at around 35°. On the other side of the Tarn both elephants and wannabe gazelles are perched on a steeper slope leading up to the peaks of performance – this slope may well be 65° (see Figure 6.10). Thus the Gauss impact curves of the Monte Carlo balls curves will be distorted and the approximate extent of this skewing is shown in Figure 8.3.

As Figure 8.3 shows, companies showing a low percent of use of innovation (i.e. being on the left, Dickensian, side of the J-curve) can profitably use multi-specialized individuals in middle management and indeed things may seem to get quite a lot better (remember the vertical axis is value) as the organization opens up to innovation and change. However, as they proceed along the skewed Gauss curve they approach a precipitous cliff and losing their footing here will hurl them into the icy waters of the Tarn of Knowledge Valley. This is a bit like oiling your trusty rusty bicycle ... a short gain before the oiling provokes a final breakdown. This is reminiscent of Saab who started applying (and really emphasized)

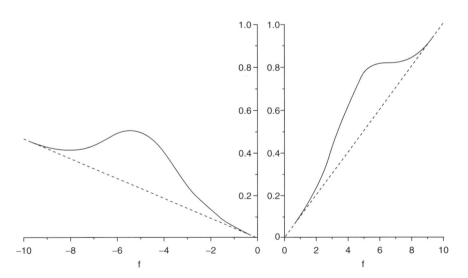

Figure 8.3 **The impact of spontaneous knowledge trails formed by overlapping nodes in areas to the left and right of the J-curve (i.e. possible effect on innovation and thus, by implication, value, of a multi-skilled middle management layer).**

BOOSTING FACTORS • FACTORS THAT STOP INNOVATION • A SUMMARY OF LESSONS LEARNT FROM KVT • RECOMBINING KNOWLEDGE AND LEARNING PROVOKES INSPIRATION • SOME CONCLUSIONS AND SUMMING UP • CHOOSING POSSIBLE TECHNOLOGIES • CALCULATE YOUR BENEFIT • LARGER ORGANIZATIONS

8   87

workplace TQM in the early 1980s with initial wins, but subsequent losses lead to them being acquired by General Motors around a decade later. So SME owners must be aware and at this point owners should decide either to scramble back up (are the casino winnings enough, or shall we continue playing Monte Carlo roulette?), or to slide down the value slope in an optimized value strategy and hope fervently to re-emerge in a BPR-type fashion on the other shore? This is tough decision, and owners may try to minimize risk by reaching decisions using widely available tools, e.g. the Mintzberg cube (Mintzberg, 1988) or other methods (see e.g. Vyakarnham & Leppard, 1999). Believe it or not, owners reaching this point may in fact be in a good position to take the plunge, because in Chapter 6, section 6.2.2 we guesstimated a value of minus 40−5=35% on the depth of the Tarn, so if the total addition to value caused by adding the new knowledge trail exceeds 35%, then there is at least a sporting chance that an enterprise of size 200 employees can succeed in crossing the Tarn of Knowledge Valley to the farther shore and may not expire in the bankrupting depths (of course, they will also be totally exposed to factors outside their control, the 'tides' while doing so). Individual companies contemplating this step should remember that their 'personal' J-curve may differ from the general model presented here (e.g. completely re-tooling a large production line will considerably add to cost, deepening their particular Tarn), but their curve can always be calculated using e.g. Cartesian or Fibonacci equations as explained in Chapter 6, section 6.2.1. There is more on this topic in Chapter 15.

Figure 8.3 also shows that companies showing a high percent of use of innovation (i.e. being on the right of the J-curve) can likewise profitably use multi-specialized individuals in middle management. The model indicates that only low or no risk is associated with this strategy and, if it works, things may get much better very rapidly indeed. After this gain in value is realized, added value will reach a drained plateau and level off. But unfortunately when the plateau is reached, developing more multi-skilled knowledge trails, or increasing the numbers/density of multi-skilled individuals (i.e. hiring more) on existing knowledge trails, should not have much further effect. In order to increase value even further new knowledge trails higher up the salary scale will have to be created. This could involve for example novel cross combinations (e.g. task forces, see Chapter 8.3) at the highest management levels.

As a last experiment the effect of bunching multi-skilled individuals on the knowledge trail was examined. Clustering overlapping nodes only in the down-stream half of the trail had only a very weak effect ($\sigma > 3$) because Monte Carlo balls were already well diffused around the DI net and only those few that hit the knowledge trail could be captured. Clustering overlapping nodes only in the upstream half of the trail had a somewhat stronger effect ($\sigma > 2$) because Monte Carlo balls were captured into the knowledge trail trajectory early, were (so to speak) on the right path and were only randomly scattered during the latter part of the DI net. Since the length of the valley can also be seen as chronological (i.e. on a time scale as the companies develop and evolve from mice at time point zero) it is tempting to speculate that these results mean that employing multi-skilled individuals early on in company development has a slightly more lasting beneficial effect than piling them in later on top of a previous generation of less innovative middle management. Certainly it should be easier to switch from the Dickensian side of the Tarn to the high-performance side at an early developmental stage, when the waters are only ankle-deep and switching costs are minimal. To put it succinctly: early mistakes may prove complicated to undo and thus have a long-lasting and costly aftermath.

8.2 Very close connections

There are many ways of tightening the links between nodes and the value of 'social glue' like e.g. Xmas parties for employees is well known, indeed over 30 years ago Allen (1977) showed that the key players in the Apollo program were those who were both in formal information management positions, but were also well connected in the social structure of the organization. However, from the point of view of the modelling presented here, even closer connections are meant. These could be e.g. family ties, which allow participants to exchange information over a long time and during many more hours than just working hours. Such links could be represented as in Figure 8.4:

Figure 8.4 **A representation of a very close connection between two nodes (i.e. representing two socially connected individuals).**

As Figure 8.4 shows, this represents a slightly looser connection than shown for the multi-skilled in Figure 8.1. There are at least two ways to encourage such closer relationships:

1. Nepotism
2. Encouraging marriage-like relationships between employees.

Nepotism is usually frowned upon when seen in competition to meritocracy-oriented mechanisms (e.g. Mellor, 2003a, 2008). However it often occurs in SMEs, in forms ranging from grooming the bosses son to take over the family business, to the Ahlstom Corporation of Finland, which reportedly employs over 200 family members (Magretta, 1998).

Before going further let me state that I, personally, am not in favour of conscious company policies in either of these two directions[3] and that they are used here purely for modelling purposes and because they are relevant to knowledge management issues, as they imply an effect on the trust and altruism factors mentioned in Chapter 2, section 2.2.

As for marriage, demographics show clearly that workers are getting married later in life and divorcing more frequently. Work is now the place where most people spend the bulk of their time and feel the greatest community. Thus the workplace is the largest source of spouses and anecdotal evidence has been presented by e.g. careerjournal.com which implies that some employers are even beginning to run marital advice clinics for their employees. So to avoid confusion, here we are not talking about married people generally (married meaning in any kind of intimate partnership, which may well add emotional stability per se), but only those cases where both individuals work reasonably closely together and – most importantly – in the same organization.

From the point of view of modelling innovation, nodes with very close connections should behave in a similar fashion to overlapping nodes (see Chapter 8, section 8.1), i.e. randomly distributing them around the DI net should make no difference, while streaming them into middle-management knowledge trails should make drumlins that are only slightly more diffuse than those caused by the multi-skilled. However the density of very closely connected nodes needed to make an appreciable difference in innovation achievement is very high in a knowledge trail (as opposed to every other for the multi-skilled). Furthermore, with very closely connected nodes due to marriage, there is actually no rationale for placing the very closely connected nodes on a linear knowledge trail corresponding to a salary level. If you remember, the multi-skilled (see Chapter 8, section 8.1) were placed on a knowledge trails on either side of the Tarn because we could reasonably assume that individuals with two or more vocational or academic degrees would be in middle management and that we could use this – translating it into value (salary) terms – to predict the band of altitude of the knowledge trail above Tarn level. In marriage terms, incomes may be wildly different and assuming parity is difficult. Certainly linking nodes at unequal heights may lead to distortions in the DI net which, being statistically random, may have unpredictable outcomes unless some form of regulatory mechanism is introduced (here I am thinking of the older Japanese model of a male worker asking his boss about the suitability of

---

[3] Personally, nepotism in my hypothetical company would mean I would run out of relatives while still a micro-organization – I only have 2 children so my nepotistic company could never grow to even 'small' size! Conversely, given the gender breakdown in many organizations (especially public organizations), encouraging marriage would imply introducing polyandry as an organizational priority. I'm not sure that will succeed!

a female co-worker as a bride, or indeed seeking an opinion as to which co-worker may be suitable. However, love marriages in Japan have outnumbered arranged marriages since 1967. For a general background on this very interesting phenomenon, see Kelly, 1991).

This opens the prospect that very closely connected nodes due to marriage may actually have negative effects on innovation. In an un-sourced quote in career-journal.com, 46% of Human Resource Management professionals and 56% of employees were reported to have the opinion that it is a good idea to talk to the new couple in order to avoid problems and the quotes presented include, 'Tension and the charged atmosphere can become so intense that you simply dread going into work every day – along with the rest of your staff' and further 'Other staff may notice that one or another of the happy couple enjoys some unfair advantage or advancement. Then you have a staff-wide issue, some grumbling, and also potential grounds for employee discrimination suits'.

In Chapter 8, section 8.1 some nodes were made double nodes to indicate multi-specialists, but the distance between a double-node and single-node neighbours was kept constant because a multi-specialist has normal transaction costs in communicating with others. But is this true for communication between married nodes and either single nodes or other married nodes?

Trust and altruism were mentioned as important factors (especially in SMEs) in Chapter 2, section 2.2 and it is quite clear that if forming very closely connected nodes due to marriage damage the trust and altruism relationship to other employees (there are hints of married couples having a hidden agenda; other commonly heard terms include 'bedroom management practices', insider trading on office politics, etc.), then these basic tenants will be negated. This adds a new degree of complexity to the DI fold which we call the Knowledge Valley because up to now it has been assumed that the DI net consists of equally spaced nodes all having equal relationships with each other. Inclusivity (as in multi-specialists) makes the net denser and thus more efficient, but exclusion is also possible, thus:

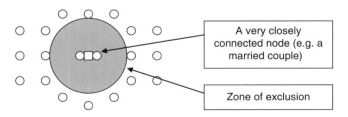

Figure 8.5 ***Illustrating the strain on the DI net incurred when a very closely connected node has an excluding relationship with surrounding nodes.***

Having 'holes' in the net, the kind of 'gravity well' depicted in Figure 8.5, is hard to represent on the already 3D Knowledge Valley. Nonetheless we can calculate approximately the effect (see Figure 8.6). The assumptions made are:

1. Monte Carlo balls double the difficulty taken to traverse paths between very closely connected nodes and other nodes (equivalent to doubling the distance – one could instead double the time, but that is nonsense in this computer model as the final time is the scatter plot completion time).
2. The zone of exclusion is circular, i.e. there is no alignment with what may loosely be called 'the aims of the organization'.
3. Very closely connected nodes are spread randomly across the DI net.

Then any effect can be seen as the number of very closely connected nodes (as percent of total number of nodes) is increased. Note that percentages have to be differentially adjusted on a sliding scale since 100% of nodes can be in very closely connected nodes, but conversely no more than 50% of very closely connected nodes can be achieved. To put that plainly, discounting polyandry, polygamy and other forms of bigamy, there will normally be two people in a marriage, so that when the number of marriages is 50% of employee number, then 100% of employees will have been accounted for.

Figure 8.6 shows the detrimental effect of having couples working in the same department. Certainly figures above 10% (2 persons together in every 10 employees) can have a very significant effect and reversing this ratio (2 singles in every 10 employees) would be expected to decimate profitability.

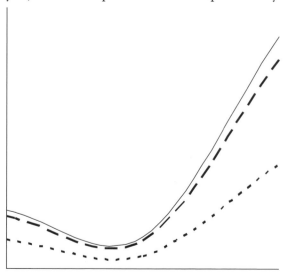

Figure 8.6 **The J-curve as in Figure 6.10, adding the effects seen for 10% of very closely connected nodes (dashed line) and 40% of very closely connected nodes (dotted line) on DI number.**

While Figure 8.6 shows the effect of adding percentages of very closely connected nodes, however it should be noted that very significant exceptions can exist. In the model presented in Figure 8.6 one assumption was that the zone of exclusion is circular and that there was thus no alignment between the aims of the couple and what may loosely be called 'the aims of the organization'. This may not be always true, exceptions may include e.g.:

A. Truly massive nepotism (see e.g. Magretta, 1998) may (re-)align the aims of the company with those of the very closely connected nodes, i.e. the company becomes subsumed into a vehicle for the families involved.
B. Other alignment with what may loosely be called 'the aims of the organization' e.g. it is the owners that are the married couple and the aims of their partnership determine the aims of the firm. Such a constellation may actually be beneficial because it could help alleviate information overload by sharing the number of nodes attaching to each person (Figure 8.7):

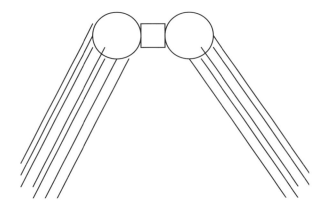

Figure 8.7 **Very closely connected nodes may protect each other from information overload and enable the joint node to increase its communicative capacity.**

The question is, how to generate or improve upon these connections in a socially acceptable manner to the advantage of the organization without incurring overload or incursion of privacy (in both the practical sense as well as the legal sense)? In the following chapter we look at some commonly seen incidences.

8.3   Task forces

Task forces are traditionally formed across co-workers and the classical typology names four forms:

A. Team structure where employees remain within department structure.

B. Lightweight team structure where employees remain within department structure but a project manager provides cross-functional integration.

C. Heavyweight team structure where employees are co-located, but still report to department managers.

D. Autonomous team structure where employees are co-located and report to project manager only.

These forms are shown in Figure 8.8, A–D, where A in the list above corresponds to A in the figure, B in the list corresponds to B in the figure and so on.

What Figure 8.8 illustrates – in terms of Knowledge Valley Theory – is the formation of 'knowledge trails'; preferred relationships in the DI node net which

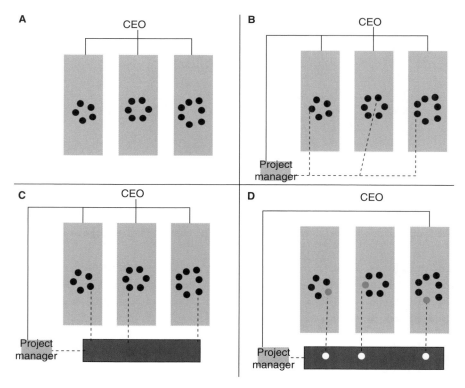

Figure 8.8 **Diagrammatical representation of the four forms of task force manage- ment where the grey columns represent departments (reporting via intermediary management to the CEO) and the dots represent employees (team members) within each department.**

forms the weft and weave of the valley structure (see Figure 6.16). However, while the knowledge trail, consisting of a specific interlinking of those thought able to perform a certain task (hence the name 'task force'), may increase the ability of the company to focus on solving the problem at hand, the formation of a task force itself will not increase DI number per se.[4] It may seem obvious, but the reason is because the DI number for these employees has already been counted so if there is any effect of task force formation upon DI number, it is, paradoxically, to reduce it in the case of autonomous team structure (case D). This is perhaps a reason why forming truly autonomous task forces should be treated with caution.

However, not all is lost. As Figure 8.8 also shows, task force recommendations go up from the project manager to the CEO and down again to the departmental managers who – presumably – implement some form of change or improvement. This gives rise to speculation that the performance of high-level management task forces could be expected to be better in terms of creating/identifying and responding to innovation. While mathematically this would again suffer from the limitations described for having 'normal employees' as part of the task force (as described above), it could lead to qualitative improvements, including:

- The improved immediacy and acceptability of any changes due to early management buy-in as stakeholders.
- Improve the quality of the information gateways ('information gatekeepers', the middle management), as these have previously been identified as important potential bottlenecks (see Chapter 3, section 3.5).
- Increased possibility of prompt diffusion from line managers and prompt implementation by subordinates.

Therefore the effect of the formation of high-level management task forces would be to improve interdepartmental communication and increase the strength of the fabric of the Knowledge Valley by increasing the density of the DI net. One further beneficial knock-on consequence could be raising the level of the troughs in the DI growth curve (Figure 6.12).

---

[4] However it is possible that those individuals involved will become better linked by extending their networks through other (ex)participants – especially by 'weak ties' (see Chapter 11, section 11.1) – and thus become 'more innovative' after the dissolution of the task force.

GENERAL INTRODUCTION • INTRODUCTION TO KNOWLEDGE MANAGEMENT •
CTION TO INNOVATION • INTRODUCTION TO ENTREPRENEURSHIP • INTRODUCTION
CONSTRUCTING KNOWLEDGE VALLEY • MANAGING FORMAL KNOWLEDGE • USING
KVT TO IDENTIFY INNOVATION BOOSTING FACTORS • FACTORS THAT STOP INNOVATION
• A SUMMARY OF LESSONS LEARNT FROM KVT. • RECOMBINING KNOWLEDGE AND
LEARNING PROVOKES INSPIRATION. • SOME CONCLUSIONS AND SUMMING UP • CHOOSING
POSSIBLE TECHNOLOGIES • CALCULATE YOUR BENEFIT • LARGER ORGANIZATIONS

9 factors that stop innovation

Clearly for DI to work one individual with a work problem has to communicate with another one who – mostly unwittingly – has an answer, leading to an 'inspiration' event. Thus one can pose the question what happens when the partner in conversation does not possess the fragment of knowledge needed? Perhaps the DI nodes are not encountered (due e.g. to departmentalization, in which case the DI number suffers, see Figure 6.12) or that the nodes encountered are inexperienced? DeLong (2004) has described the 'Lost Knowledge' phenomenon of senior and very knowledgeable workers retiring in demographically serious numbers. In theoretical terms and at a meta-level this should not influence competitiveness, because in general throughout the economy all organizations should be equally affected. However on a specific micro-level it is obvious that some organizations depend on knowledge more than others. These organizations may not be clustered in high-tech sectors and indeed e.g. real estate, stock broking and other 'conventional' areas rely heavily on accumulated knowledge and experience.

9.1 Rifts: Leadership Mentality

Management style has already been touched on in Chapter 5 and includes the Covin and Slevin classification of SMEs (Covin & Slevin, 1998; Slevin & Covin, 1990). It seems clear that the apparent distance between nodes (and thus the difficulty in traversing this portion of a knowledge trail) can be increased if one individual perceives the other as unapproachable, less of a colleague. Perhaps the most important distinction of this type is between worker and manager (Figure 9.1).

Thus fair working norms are established and the DI net grows denser if both manager and worker perceive themselves as e.g. scientists or marketers and mutual respect plays down the differences in their functions (i.e. level) within the organization. Such leaders will often also better understand the work being done, exemplify key values and are more likely to be consistent, to provide resources

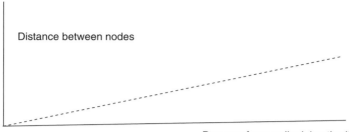

Distance between nodes

Degree of non-collegial authority

Figure 9.1 **Reluctance to communicate with leaders (perceived distance between nodes) as a function of the degree of difference in formal authority between communicators. The extreme left could represent a leader who is an authority (i.e. expert) in the relevant field and on the extreme right a leader who is not knowledgeable about the subject matter, but possesses the same degree of decision-making powers (i.e. has authority) as the expert leader.**

(realistic time and financial budgets), motivation (also at strategic level) and generally 'walk the talk'.

There is general agreement that knowledge workers are not motivated primarily by money, but by an inner need for achievement and the feeling that they have 'made a mark', including recognition from peers and superiors. To do this they need time and space to explore and create in safety; i.e. to be able to 'fail' and still be rewarded for having tried. The seminal publication by Tampoe (1993) identifies four key motivators for knowledge workers:

1. personal growth
2. operational autonomy
3. task achievement
4. money and other rewards

However four 'static' factors can be misleading and indeed it is probable that knowledge workers have different priorities as their career develops (somewhat akin to a 'Product Life Cycle' alluded to previously) and it may well be that e.g. climbing the career ladder is also a factor for younger individuals, but data is lacking and only the diffuse guidelines given above are generally accepted. Leaders and managers with an insight into what this involves on both group and individual basis will be far more successful than managers who do not understand the subject matter and instead rely on formal authority. 'Best practice' management is a term often bandied around and interested readers are encouraged to compare and contrast 'best practice' with 'best fit' perspectives (see Hansen et al. 1999 and other authors).

BOOSTING FACTORS · **FACTORS THAT STOP INNOVATION** · A SUMMARY OF LESSONS LEARNT FROM KVT · RECOMBINING KNOWLEDGE AND LEARNING PROVOKES INSPIRATION · SOME CONCLUSIONS AND SUMMING UP · CHOOSING POSSIBLE TECHNOLOGIES · CALCULATE YOUR BENEFIT · LARGER ORGANIZATIONS

9

97

In addition to individual relationships between managers and workers, the DI net can become strained between groups – managers as a group and workers as a group, and this will be considered in section 9.2.

9.2   Impermeable leadership strata

Unfortunate situations can arise when a whole strata or layer of non-knowledge workers start managing knowledge work. Starbuck (1992) pointed out that knowledge intensive organizations lose credibility when support staff come to functionally or numerically outnumber experts. Indeed as long ago as 1979, Mintzberg (1979) foresaw that knowledge-intensive organizations will inevitably evolve into professional bureaucracies. One example of this is in higher education where administrative and support staff tend to outnumber (both in number and resources used) academic staff by around 3:2. This is what Deem et al. (2007) have called the 'Divided University'. A rift in the DI net springs from the higher transaction costs for communication between those who in a university environment may consider themselves 'academic colleagues' and those who are their lower qualified managers. Academics can in time come to regard themselves as being milked and herded by an overblown and semi-parasitic bureaucracy. Anecdotal evidence suggests that this effect is not confined to universities and may contribute to inefficiency in e.g. the National Health Service, where a class of professional administrators are now doing the leadership jobs once performed by medically trained staff.

It is a moot point if Knowledge Valley Theory – which explicitly is about SMEs – can be applied to universities (or the National Health Service). However universities consist (largely) of a collection of faculties, and these – to some extent – are self-managed units of some 100–200 staff and thus, viewed from a certain perspective, universities (i.e. a collection of faculties) could be regarded as a collection of SMEs. The critical reader could regard this as a tenuous argument, but I am going to use it anyway to justify including the following paragraph in this book.

Since salaries can be placed on the J-curve and administrative staff – especially in public services – tend to have similar pay, then professional administrators can be seen to behave as an impermeable geological strata in the knowledge valley, a layer of unforgiving granite or slippery clay where footholds are few and far between. Knowledge workers will have difficulty following knowledge trails through this rock face and thus knowledge trails linking the DI net above and below the administrative layer will become attenuated or even terminated. The consequences will be to lower the average (attainable) height of the peaks of performance. In the short term those with a self-sustaining DI net can exist above the administrative layer – these may be the 'star researchers' bought in by universities for their research history, but in fact such star researchers exist in only tenuous contact with their more teaching-oriented colleagues in the organization. This situation can continue for as long as peak performers can be imported from outside the organization. However if the effect continues for a sufficient length of time, long enough to be sufficient for the supply of peak performers to dry up, then the peaks will erode and the right-hand side of the J-curve will diminish to the maximum set by the impermeable strata, i.e. that side of Knowledge Valley will be a flat plateau at a level approximating to the administrative strata.

GENERAL INTRODUCTION • INTRODUCTION TO KNOWLEDGE MANAGEMENT • CTION TO INNOVATION • INTRODUCTION TO ENTREPRENEURSHIP • INTRODUCTION CONSTRUCTING KNOWLEDGE VALLEY • MANAGING FORMAL KNOWLEDGE • USING KVT TO IDENTIFY INNOVATION BOOSTING FACTORS • FACTORS THAT STOP INNOVATION • A SUMMARY OF LESSONS LEARNT FROM KVT • RECOMBINING KNOWLEDGE AND LEARNING PROVOKES INSPIRATION • SOME CONCLUSIONS AND SUMMING UP • CHOOSING POSSIBLE TECHNOLOGIES • CALCULATE YOUR BENEFIT • LARGER ORGANIZATIONS

10 a summary of lessons learnt from KVT

In this chapter I will briefly sum up some of the more novel or overlooked findings which Knowledge Valley Theory has indicated may be useful to management science, Knowledge Management and Information Systems – especially where these intersect with research on small businesses.

10.1 SME management

Diversity innovation, process innovation, incremental innovation and so on are all terms used to describe how progress (and thus presumably, growth) is made in SMEs. If employees are to continue to provide mutual inspiration ('good ideas') to each other, then the size of their immediate environment – in terms of the numbers of co-workers with which they can communicate – is of paramount importance. The transaction costs for communicating to too many become unbearable at an employee number of approximately 50. Around this size, management changes are forced onto SMEs and this is a hypercritical time for them (and totally overlooked by classical business studies research) because failing to adapt correctly to this new management challenge will cripple a growing SME. Mistakes made at this stage can not only be costly in terms of money, but also in terms of the time needed to recognize and correct the situation. This is the first of two major challenges for a growing SME; the second being around the 90–110 employees stage and involves departmentalization and possibly the decision to seek external investment to support further expansion. A third capping stage is obviously inevitable, but is not explored here further, because it exceeds the definition of SMEs, by launching them into being large companies (see Chapter 14).

10.2 SME evolution and levering DI number

Utterback (1994 and see Figure 3.3) shows that the value of an invention is seriously augmented by knowledge of implementation. In SMEs inventions are few and far between, so implementation becomes of overarching and paramount importance. As argued in Chapter 3, the type of innovation promoting implementation and processes is a kind of mutual inspiration called 'diversity innovation' (see Figure 3.1) it is of the utmost importance that companies – probably through business-oriented Information Systems – are able to lever this factor. Those that can are well on the way to becoming gazelles (although this cannot be construed as a guarantee), whether they have formal intellectual property, or not. Certainly companies not able – or willing – to lever their innovation capacities or DI number, are unlikely to become gazelles.

10.3 Departmentalization

As was illustrated in Chapter 6, section 6.1.4, to maximize DI, employers should not fragment the company too early and should also strive to keep the size of their departments as large as possible. In all departments open communication should be an explicit responsibility for everyone, as this will make achieving maximum DI easier. Where smaller departments are unavoidable – e.g. overseas offices – these should be 'seeded' with employees taken from the larger departments. Furthermore the 'information gatekeepers' stationed between departments (normally the head of department), should ensure that his or her department has good communications with the others (i.e. ensure that the departmental DI is available to the company generally). Certainly secretive or biased persons should never be allowed positions as 'information gatekeepers' and should this become apparent, then these interface problems must be tackled swiftly by an impartial leader. Trust is a very important factor in Knowledge Management in SMEs and trust-destroying measures – departmental politics or other middle management petty squabbles – are especially damaging because they function at the 'information gatekeeper' level. Blocking clear communication channels at this level can easily decimate DI number.

10.4 Multi-specialists in low-innovation environments

Simply relaxing conditions in 'Dickensian' low-innovation companies (i.e. those on the left of the J-curve) without a clear strategy may paradoxically leave the company floundering (see Chapter 6, section 6.2.5). Clearly, unifying several smaller rigid management hierarchies with poor communication into one despotic monolithic rigid management hierarchy with poor communication will theoretically increase the DI number but not actual 'shop floor' performance. The overall effect will be to decrease value and earnings as the company slips towards the right of the J-curve, towards the Tarn. If, however, a clear strategic decision has been taken to improve innovation (by e.g. amalgamating departments), such companies can profitably use multi-specialized and/or ex-pat and so on individuals in middle management, providing that the skills brought in, and the innovations generated, are in close alignment with the company's core competencies (Quinn & Hilmer, 1995). If this can be achieved, Figure 8.3 shows that the company's general health may improve considerably. As the organization opens up to innovation, the strategic choices for the leadership are either to watch and control this process carefully, or to deliberately plunge through a BPR-type transformation into a high-innovation organization.

10.5 Multi-specialists in high-innovation environments

Companies approaching gazelle-like status (i.e. those on the right of the J-curve) can likewise profitably use multi-specialized, ex-pat and other such individuals in middle management. The model indicates that only low or no risk is associated with this strategy and, if it works, the innovation status may improve very rapidly indeed. However this effect is not infinitely recyclable and after a point packing more and more multi-specialized, ex-pat and other similar individuals into middle management will bring ever-diminishing returns. Usually it is a requirement that any new innovations generated should be in alignment with the company's core competencies (Quinn & Hilmer, 1995). However in this case one may suspect that this requirement could be relaxed somewhat as the high-innovation environment will presumably be relatively open for, and supportive of, incentives involving corporate entrepreneurship (intrapreneurship) and spinning-out those innovations which the parent company cannot properly lever. This does not need to be in a high-tech environment:

Case 8

Corporate entrepreneurship – intrapreneurship

In one Danish travel company in 1998 several older employees refused to start using computers, so, realizing these individuals had both a useful skills set as well as a rapport with some customers, 'senior travel' was spun out. This intrapreneurial initiative had classical Schumpeterian effects, reaping high but transient rewards (transient until the individuals involved reached pension age) and indeed has subsequently been copied successfully elsewhere.

Thus introducing an innovative middle management layer can be especially fruitful if the parent company is genuinely entrepreneurial or at least open to intrapreneurial initiatives.

102   10

GENERAL INTRODUCTION · INTRODUCTION TO KNOWLEDGE MANAGEMENT · INTRODUCTION TO INNOVATION · INTRODUCTION TO ENTREPRENEURSHIP · INTRODUCTION TO SMES · CONSTRUCTING KNOWLEDGE VALLEY · MANAGING FORMAL KNOWLEDGE · USING KVT TO IDENTIFY INNOVATION

10.6   Family relationships

Unless the aims of a married couple are aligned with the aims of the company (e.g. they are the owners), then marriage (as defined in Chapter 8, section 8.2) can be tolerated up to a level around approximately 10% of employee number. Above that figure company performance slips significantly due to an exclusion zone around each double node, and this is especially damaging as there is no way back – couples cannot be expected to divorce and re-take-up their previous behaviour for the good of the company. Exceptions to this general scenario could be massive nepotism (see e.g. Magretta, 1998) where in fact the company ceases to be primarily market-oriented and instead becomes a vehicle for the family. Indeed while not wishing to imply any link between Finland and inbreeding, I would indeed be interested to know how a company with 200 family members (Magretta, 1998) handles workplace romance. Otherwise nepotism, except for valid purposes, e.g. succession planning in a family-run company, should be discouraged (see e.g. Mellor, 2003a).

10.7   Task forces

Task forces are specifically focused knowledge trails and are aimed at solving a particular problem. They do not increase DI number although they may have other side effects, e.g. fully autonomous task forces may decrease DI number, or that individuals once involved in task forces may subsequently become crystallization nuclei for innovation once the task force has been dissolved but weak ties (see Chapter 11, section 11.1) remain. Novel task forces that cross combinations at the highest management levels can also be created. Such high-level management task forces are likely to improve innovation not by increasing the DI number, but by thickening the DI net. Since this effect would have a particularly noticeable positive influence on raising the level of the troughs in the DI growth curve (Figure 6.12), it may be that forming such management task forces may be particularly appropriate during and immediately after the formation of new departments.

10.8   After work: Seniors

High-quality knowledge is continually leaking out of organizations as their most experienced staff retire and this should be considered a disadvantage, at least in the short term. However this knowledge can still be accessed (i.e. the extent of the DI net can be artificially expanded) by retaining loose relationships with retirees, whether by largely mundane low-cost methods like organizations forming a 'pensioners club' and inviting members to the Xmas party, or by more complex, structured, means e.g. re-hiring retired staff on a temp basis. Universities already do this at a low level by organizing alumni and at a much higher level by using the 'emeritus' system.

GENERAL INTRODUCTION • INTRODUCTION TO KNOWLEDGE MANAGEMENT •
O INNOVATION • INTRODUCTION TO ENTREPRENEURSHIP • INTRODUCTION
RUCTING KNOWLEDGE VALLEY • MANAGING FORMAL KNOWLEDGE • USING
KVT TO IDENTIFY INNOVATION BOOSTING FACTORS • FACTORS THAT STOP INNOVATION
• A SUMMARY OF LESSONS LEARNT FROM KVT • RECOMBINING KNOWLEDGE AND
LEARNING PROVOKES INSPIRATION • SOME CONCLUSIONS AND SUMMING UP • CHOOSING
POSSIBLE TECHNOLOGIES • CALCULATE YOUR BENEFIT • LARGER ORGANIZATIONS

Part IV building applied information Systems

Context and aims

Up to now we have (hopefully) enjoyed a wide and amusing trip around the theories of how to grow organizations using the abstract principles of Knowledge Management as modified by those of Innovation and Entrepreneurship. But reality is a harsh mistress: how do we implement what we have seen? There is no one answer or at least none that fits all (much to the disconcertment of CMS/CRM providers, Open Source or not), but the following section explores some characteristics that effective Information Systems – by virtue of the preceding body of text – should (or could) exhibit.

Obviously the actual software will change with time; I can only hope that implementers will heed the lesson of Figure 12.2. The actual implementation and what this consists of is up to the artistry, skill and understanding of the consultant involved.

At the end of this chapter the reader should be able to competently account for types of technologies that could be used in implementing IT-mediated Information Systems that are 'fit for purpose' from a Knowledge Management perspective.

GENERAL INTRODUCTION • INTRODUCTION TO KNOWLEDGE MANAGEMENT • CTION TO INNOVATION • INTRODUCTION TO ENTREPRENEURSHIP • INTRODUCTION • CONSTRUCTING KNOWLEDGE VALLEY • MANAGING FORMAL KNOWLEDGE • USING KVT TO IDENTIFY INNOVATION BOOSTING FACTORS • FACTORS THAT STOP INNOVATION • A SUMMARY OF LESSONS LEARNT FROM KVT • RECOMBINING KNOWLEDGE AND LEARNING PROVOKES INSPIRATION • SOME CONCLUSIONS AND SUMMING UP • CHOOSING POSSIBLE TECHNOLOGIES • CALCULATE YOUR BENEFIT • LARGER ORGANIZATIONS

11 recombining knowledge and learning provokes inspiration

Until now the KVT model has worked on the following assumptions:

1. A person can have a very large number of ties and that there is no upper limit.
2. All ties are exactly similar and have the same 'weight', quality and importance independent of their length.

These have been stated in Chapter 6 and especially in Figure 6.3. The only deviation from these principles has been in Chapter 8, section 8.2, where the effects of an exclusion zone around very closely connected nodes were looked at. Even knowledge trails do not contradict these assumptions, as they merely define and improve the direction and bandwidth of ties.

The two assumptions have allowed the creation of a nice clean and well-defined model which we can manipulate and draw general conclusions from. However these assumptions are extreme and to some extent unrealistic; workers cannot gyrate freely around their organizations chatting freely to all and sundry for days on end, and indeed even the most hardened socialite has an upper limit on how many 'ties' they can handle, both emotionally and from the point of view of information overload. When this point is reached, it becomes again the domain of Knowledge Management and business-oriented Information Systems.

11.1 What are weak ties?

According to Granovetter (1973), ties are not uniform but can have different strengths and can be approximately grouped into three categories: absent, weak or strong. The strength of an interpersonal tie is a combination of the amount of time, emotional intensity, intimacy (understood as mutually sharing confidences) and reciprocity involved. We tend to be close friends with those we have strong ties, and the information, world view and network they have corresponds closely with our own (Kirton, 2003). Thus it is acquaintances – with whom we have weak ties – that give access to more novel information, different views and new networks. Weak ties have been explored in the context of e.g. social cohesion, individual power and the spread of rumours, but not expressly in connection with innovation or with learning. Granovetter (2004) does briefly treat 'social structure and innovation' but limits himself to pointing out the importance of weak ties in connecting e.g. the technical with the financial exemplified by venture capitalists in Silicon Valley. However as Granovetter (1983) states 'weak ties provide people with access to information and resources beyond those available in their own social circle, but strong ties have greater motivation to be of assistance and are typically more easily available', so there does in fact appear to be a nice fit between Granovetters work and that presented here.

Acknowledging that, in order to fit reality more closely, that the KVT assumption on the uniformity of ties should be modified to better fit 'life', then some conclusions could face modification too. For example, the conclusion that task forces solve specific problems, but do not increase innovation: KVT implies that task force members may become crystallization nuclei for innovation after the task force has been dissolved but that without weak ties being formed with others, then task force autonomy may actually decrease overall innovation. However members of dissolved task forces will retain weak ties (if not strong ties), which will be positive, furthermore converting acquaintances into friends during a task force mission could radically increase the number of further weak ties available to the individuals involved through their new-found acquaintances and friends. Thus weak ties may well modify KVT conclusions regarding task forces.

If we understand weak ties to be conduits for ideas that are new (to those receiving them) and relevant, then Information Systems should be able to some degree to replicate this and deliver knowledge to the right target group or individual at the right time. As such, the learning theories associated with the management of knowledge assets, as expounded by Boisot (1998), are (again, see Chapter 2, section 2.1) highly relevant. Boisot is professor of strategic management in Barcelona and he distinguishes between N-learning and S-learning, S-learning being the sudden jump in understanding when things fall into place (the 'ah-ha' experience – certainly sharing some characteristics with chatting with an interesting weak tie acquaintance).

11.2   N-Learning

N-learning stands for Newtonian learning, because of its neoclassical and mechanical aspects. N-learning is the linear learning of hard, codified and abstract facts. This is the 'dry' learning contained in standard large textbooks. If the textbook is comprehensive enough and understandably written, then everyone is, or relatively easily can be, in possession of all the facts. That is, the facts are well diffused, well codified and abstract so there is nothing left to do than sit down and learn them.

11.3   S-Learning

S-learning stands for Schumpeterian learning, named after the 'economist of the entrepreneur', J. Schumpeter, who gave rise to the term 'creative destruction' (see Chapter 4, section 4.1). Boisot argues that knowledge may be progressive, i.e. subsequent approximations may lead to a better grasp of the underlying structure, but they are not necessarily cumulative, leading to one monolithic structure. On the contrary, new hypotheses often destroy old ones. S-learning thus involves a non-linear insight or a jump in understanding. A key issue here is diffusion. In S-learning the facts are less codified and less diffused.

Case 9

Effectively communicating new principles

An example of N- and S-Learning (taken from Mellor & Mellor, 2004) is:

Suppose a student has learnt both English and German. The student has read large books, visited German- and English-speaking countries, and spent time poring over thick dictionaries. This is mechanical (N-) learning.

Now suppose the same student finds out that there is a letter in Icelandic that looks like a 'd', but is pronounced 'eth'. The Icelandic for 'bath' (as in 'bath room') is 'bað', or 'BAÐ', pronounced 'baeth'. Obviously, in English, the sound is similar (bath) and thus the letters are now TH. However, in German, the letter (Ð) has been 'mutated' to a D and the sound changed accordingly (the German for 'bath' is 'bad', where the 'd' is very definitely a 'D' sound). By realizing this connection the student has built upon the two solid legs of N-learning (years of learning English and German) and is able to experience a flash of insight. This is the jump in understanding that is typical of S-learning. Usually this 'ah-ha' experience will stimulate the student to further renew their efforts (in this case, in the Germanic languages).

However S-learning may often contain a component of N-learning. Indeed N-learning is fractal. One could consider in the above example that the blocks of N-learning were not at all the fundamental blocks, but that they in turn rest upon the N-learning involved in learning to speak, to read and to write. This cyclical nature of the Boisot model is reminiscent of Argyris's works on single- and double-loop learning (see e.g. Argyris & Schön, 1974). Interested readers are also referred to Salomon (1979) who mentions 'user situation', 'technology', 'content' and 'symbolic system' as critical success factors in technology-driven learning systems (those with an interest in education may also like to peruse Mellor & Mellor, 2004, or, for a more recent overview and discussion, the many works of Peter Jarvis for an in-depth analysis).

Clearly there are implications here for Information Systems: To continue the case example above, Information Systems can only contribute marginally to the N-learning of German by providing on-line newspapers and searchable dictionaries on CD. The S-learning is much more amenable to digital techniques; not only comparative or etymological as in the example, but also in the form of e.g. quizzes or crossword puzzles for repetition, 'learning-by-doing' and 'theory-in-use', resulting in increased effectiveness and better acceptance of failures and mistakes.

11.4 Learning and pedagogical aspects of information systems

Research into educational psychology has delivered several theories of how adults learn. Indeed, as far as Information Systems in the UK is concerned, a very large body of work has been developed by the Joint Information Systems Committee (JISC, available at jisc.ac.uk). There are various typologies of learning and Table 11.1 shows the four major perspectives commonly held to pertain to adult learning.

There is a burgeoning literature connected with educational theory and this is not the place to cut through it. Mellor and Mellor (2004) skim through

Table 11.1 **Four perspectives of learning and their associated pedagogies.**

Perspective	Pedagogy
Associative Perspective: Learning as acquiring competence	• Focus on competencies • Routines of organized activity • Progressive stages of difficulty • Matching goals with prior performance
Individual Constructive Perspective: Learning as achieving individual understanding	• Interactions involve knowledge building • Encourage experimentation and discovery of principles • Reflection and evaluation
Social Constructive Perspective: Learning as achieving collaborative understanding	• Interactions involve knowledge building • Activities for collaboration and shared expression of ideas • Reflection, peer-review and evaluation
Situative Perspective: Learning as social practice	• Communities of practice to support enquiry and learning • Dialogue and honing of learning skills

the essentials, but a good primer for deeper study is Jarvis (2003) and indeed many of the other numerous works of Peter Jarvis. Those interested in educational philosophy may appreciate Dunn (2004). Despite this good theory we must ask, this was developed for schools and higher education settings, however Business-oriented Information Systems is not education. Differences are that in our setting we wish to help staff to retrieve information, see connections and learn rapidly, but we do not aim to help them dispute, revise or to sit exams. Nonetheless we can easily imagine that in one organization, two people may be asking the same question, but one will want 'the short answer' while the other may want exhaustive details, i.e. that these two people are at different knowledge levels. Therefore which bits of these educational theories do we take to make focussed Information Systems for business (i.e. aligned with the organizations direction or core competencies)?

Clearly increasing throughput on the Social Learning Cycle is an important part of Knowledge Management and extremely relevant for Business-oriented Information Systems. However the SLC is also not a conveyer belt that all and sundry can jump on with equal success: The brothers Hubert and Stuart Dreyfus say in the Dreyfus Model of Skills Acquisition (Dreyfus & Dreyfus, 1986) that many of our skills are acquired at an early age by trial and error or by imitation, but that adults learn new skills by instruction. These instructional levels can be broken down as given in Table 11.2:

Although Dreyfus and Dreyfus show how to focus on educational levels, they do not reveal how content should be presented. Another factor that the Dreyfus brothers fail to mention is regression. Those doing beginner courses corresponding to Stages 1, 2 and perhaps a little of stage 3, will quickly regress if they fail to practice and they will go down in competence unless reinforcement takes place. Indeed research and experience show that students re-taking a course exam even only six months later will score significantly less than they originally did if they have not used their knowledge in the intervening time (see double-loop learning e.g. Argyris & Schön, 1974). There exists a huge amount of literature on this subject, which goes way beyond the scope of this book, but the interested reader may also like to look up the classical works by Kolb and by Jarvis.

Thus the overarching prerequisites for increasing throughput in the Social Learning Cycle start to become clearer (see also Chapter 12, section 12.2). Especially for IT-driven systems these include:

1. promoting weak ties to other people and also to other topics
2. putting more weight on S-learning than N-learning
3. carefully gauging the learning level of the user

Obviously if the users are proficient or even more expert, then IT-driven systems will hardly be able to add to their knowledge. For them, the actual and real

Table 11.2 **A brief synopsis of skills levels according to the Dreyfus Model of Skills Acquisition (Dreyfus & Dreyfus, 1986). See also Mellor & Mellor (2004).**

Stage	Description
Stage 1: Novice	The novice begins to learn to recognize objective facts and features that are relevant to the skill being learnt. One characteristic of relevant elements is that they are context-free, that is that they can be recognized without reference to the overall situation. Thus the novice acquires basic rules to follow such as mechanical IT skills.
Stage 2: Advanced beginner	The novice needs to cope with real situations and when this is achieved the advanced beginner will improve in performance. This means that the advanced beginner does not learn by rules or verbal description, but by experience. The new elements are called 'situational' because they are relevant to a specific situation. The advanced beginner can now start to make decisions regarding both the context-free and the situational elements.
Stage 3: Competent	As time goes, there is no possibility to keep all elements (both context-free and situational) in mind and indeed learners doing this will not focus on the goal. The learner needs to adopt a hierarchical procedure of decision-making. This involves the need to organize the situation, to choose a plan of attack or problem solving and then to examine a small set of factors. Accordingly the competent (with a goal in mind) begins to see a situation as a set of facts and can decide that a certain conclusion should be drawn, a decision made or expectation investigated.
Stage 4: Proficient	The proficient is deeply involved in the task, recognizing that certain features of the situation are more important than others. Because proficient people have experienced similar situations that worked in the past they are able to associate present situations and anticipate probable consequences. The proficient responds to patterns without decomposing them into components by a process of holistic discrimination and association. Proficient people can be recognized by an involved and intuitive understanding, followed by detached decision-making.
Stage 5: Expert	An expert generally knows what to do based on mature and practiced understanding. The expert does not see problems in some detached way, the skill of an expert is a part of him and he is deeply involved in coping with his environment. With rich and deep experience of a variety of situations, all can be seen from the same perspective or with the same goal in mind, but requiring different tactical decisions. With expertise comes fluid performance.

presence of a master is essential. Conversely the use of IT-driven systems can facilitate a kind of mass education, but it can only teach beginners the rules and facts that can – with repetition – make them competent in theoretical aspects, and IT-driven systems will not normally produce practical experts (or please contact me should anyone have any concrete examples).

GENERAL INTRODUCTION • INTRODUCTION TO KNOWLEDGE MANAGEMENT •
CTION TO INNOVATION • INTRODUCTION TO ENTREPRENEURSHIP • INTRODUCTION
• CONSTRUCTING KNOWLEDGE VALLEY • MANAGING FORMAL KNOWLEDGE • USING
KVT TO IDENTIFY INNOVATION BOOSTING FACTORS • FACTORS THAT STOP INNOVATION
• A SUMMARY OF LESSONS LEARNT FROM KVT • RECOMBINING KNOWLEDGE AND
LEARNING PROVOKES INSPIRATION • SOME CONCLUSIONS AND SUMMING UP • CHOOSING
POSSIBLE TECHNOLOGIES • CALCULATE YOUR BENEFIT • LARGER ORGANIZATIONS

12 some conclusions and summing up

There are unfortunately many consultants who, as the saying goes, will 'take your watch then tell you the time'. After reading this book you may also think that it has told you a lot of stuff you already know. Let's have a look at some of them, just in case you don't quite know as much as you think, but please note that these are not dichotomous opposites, many are simply extensions on common – and correct – perceptions.

12.1 General management and SMEs

Table 12.1 **Summary of some of the better and less well-known findings resulting from Knowledge Valley Theory as related to general business studies.**

	'Common knowledge'	New (or at least less common) knowledge
General company development	Get everyone together around the water cooler	Diversity innovation ('mutual inspiration' – possibly in processes) is a powerful economic driving force and especially important in SMEs, because they often lack inventions (patents, etc.)
SME development	The family (and friends) can manage everything	The first major challenge is setting up a good professional management structure at employee number ~50
SME development	Keep going until it's not fun anymore	Capping of growth occurs according to the owners personal wishes, and may occur at any (financially possible) stage
SME development	At some point new cash is going to be needed	Capping of growth according to owners personal wish to seek external capital (or not), often at employee number ~90–110.
SME management	Early mistakes in forming the management team may haunt you for an inordinate time afterwards.	These deadly early mistakes can only partially be ameliorated by employing an innovative middle management later.

Continued

Table 12.1 **Continued**

	'Common knowledge'	New (or at least less common) knowledge
Managing innovation	Let's get some fresh ideas in, that's bound to be good	'Dickensian' companies cannot randomly and rapidly open up to innovation without running the risk of spiralling into bankruptcy.
Managing innovation	The firm needs people who have grown up in the branch	Employing a multi-skilled middle management may help increase the value of non-entrepreneurial ('Dickensian') companies. This may help to the extent that the company may try (and have the resources) to consciously become entrepreneurial and innovative.
Managing innovation	Effective entrepreneurial companies' (Covin & Slevin, see Table 5.4) can somehow lever intrapreneurship	Employing a multi-skilled middle management will increase the value of entrepreneurial companies, either directly or via intrapreneurship.
Departmentalization	Encourage competition: Everyone gets their own 'little kingdom' fast and competes for resources.	Delay forming departmental divisions as long as possible and keep departments large.
Shifts	Some people are better able to cope with night work than others.	Rotate shift workers so that everyone meets everyone else. Allow telecommuting as long as it is not excessive.
Innovations	Innovations can only be in line with the companies' core competencies. (Quinn & Hilmer, 1995).	Innovations should be in line with the companies' core competencies if the company is not very entrepreneurial, but if the company is entrepreneurial, then innovations can be levered using spin-out intrapreneurship.
Innovations	Innovations will spread through a firm	The Rogers (1983) DoI model does not work well for departmentalized organizations.
Innovations	Middle managers should be free to boss their subordinates around according to circumstances, this forms a proper team.	Middle management should be well-functioning information gatekeepers and change agents in good contact with their peers and subordinates.
Managing the managers	Middle managers can see change coming and will do their best to help the firm cope.	Middle management sabotage, either directly or by inhibiting communication flow between information gatekeepers, is common and the largest obstacle to properly levering knowledge assets.

Continued

BOOSTING FACTORS • FACTORS THAT STOP INNOVATION • A SUMMARY OF LESSONS LEARNT FROM KVT • RECOMBINING KNOWLEDGE AND LEARNING PROVOKES INSPIRATION • **SOME CONCLUSIONS AND SUMMING UP** • CHOOSING POSSIBLE TECHNOLOGIES • CALCULATE YOUR BENEFIT • LARGER ORGANIZATIONS

12   115

Table 12.1 **Continued**

	'Common knowledge'	New (or at least less common) knowledge
Formation of exclusion zones	Nepotism is allowed but only for valid succession planning in family-run companies. Married owner couples make a good leadership team.	Don't let more than 1 in 9 of your employees marry each other, unless they are all in one big happy extended family and you can thus realign the company to follow family (as opposed to market) goals.
Task forces	Keep control of task forces, they may become too independent.	Task forces solve specific problems, but do not increase innovation. Members may become crystallization nuclei for innovation after the task force has been dissolved. Task force autonomy may decrease overall innovation.
Task forces	Top management doesn't need task force type organization.	Higher management task forces should be instigated during and immediately after re-organizations, especially where they have led to changes in personnel or responsibilities.
Gazelles	Mice can evolve into gazelles, the statistical frequency being ~4%	Gazelles lever innovation in all aspects of business and innovation and this is contributed to by all employees.
Mice	Mice grow all by themselves.	Mice will probably remain mice if they inhabit a mature market. Inhabiting an immature market will propel them towards being gazelles, unless they cap their innovation potential and thus evolve to elephants. 'Treading water' in an immature market will lead to failure.
Elephants	There is nothing principally wrong with being 'Newtonian' or an elephant, especially in basic markets.	Elephants can mutate into gazelles, but the creative destruction involved will probably be great.
General	In SMEs, doing a flawless job for around five years may gain you access to the management consensus group.	Trust is much more important in SMEs than in large companies, because large companies depend more on CV banks, etc.

12.2 The final version of Knowledge Valley

If you were aware of more than 10–12 of the findings above (Table 12.1), then you may classify yourself as 'pretty good'. However the use of this theory is not only that it explains all of the notions – gathered by practical experience (see the 'common knowledge' column of Table 12.1) above – but goes further and indicates guidelines that indicate genuinely new ways for companies to

GENERAL INTRODUCTION · INTRODUCTION TO KNOWLEDGE MANAGEMENT · INTRODUCTION TO INNOVATION · INTRODUCTION TO ENTREPRENEURSHIP · INTRODUCTION TO SMES · CONSTRUCTING KNOWLEDGE VALLEY · MANAGING FORMAL KNOWLEDGE · USING KVT TO IDENTIFY INNOVATION

116   12

lever their knowledge assets. As such, Knowledge Valley Theory presents a step forward and a future theoretical base for new developments, e.g. it indicates the position of social entrepreneurship (charities, etc.) and state undertakings like ministries, on the knowledge landscape. This has been made possible by unifying the previously separate academic fields of Knowledge Management and Innovation, by way of the mutually overlapping field, Entrepreneurship (Figure 1.1).

However the rarefied peak of performance as indicated in Figure 12.1 may not be attained; as we saw in Figure 8.3 the vertical axis can be equated to salary, and because conquering the peak depends on maintaining the DI number, we can ask the question: Can low-paid employees still connect to the highly paid? If not, the peak will be lower (i.e. the DI number will be less). Satisfyingly we now see in fairly abstract and theoretical terms the rationale behind TQM, quality circle and other management schemes ('flat management structure') that form conduits for information (and knowledge) from the lowly paid to high management.

Despite the fact that Knowledge Valley Theory explains so many things we know, and that it is amenable to experimentation and projections, it is too early to say what may become of the Knowledge Valley; perhaps an earthquake or a new ice age will quickly reduce it to rubble and moraine! Is there such a thing as 'knowledge tectonics' – cultural continents rubbing together and giving rise to knowledge Himalayas or Challenger Depths? Whatever... it has been fun developing even this small piece of knowledge cartography, and I hope my small insights may prove to be useful to at least a few of you.

12.3   Information Systems or Information Technology?

Although specialists in Information Systems will operate in different contexts they should understand how knowledge and information can be ordered and shared with others, i.e. becomes 'value added', contextual, relevant and actionable – subject to refinement by experience (including the experiences of others) and subject to reflection and 'learning'. I have argued in this book that more value is added if this sharing results in 'mutual inspiration'.

Data collection and storage are obvious places to start: databases and XML. This leads logically to data structures, UML, data warehousing and data mining (including SQL and x-query). To input and retrieve information, specific apps are needed; thus the practitioner should be conversant with a range of relevant protocols, programming techniques and languages. Although this admittedly may be 'programming light', they should have grasped the principles of programming and the like involved and be able to choose on a rational basis which tools are most appropriate for a set task, as well as how to accomplish a set task (i.e. Project

Performance peak

Drumlin of the
multi-skilled

Lifestyle satisfaction
base camps

Knowledge trails

Figure 12.1 **A panorama of Knowledge Valley. For the sake of clarity Dickensian side has been omitted.**

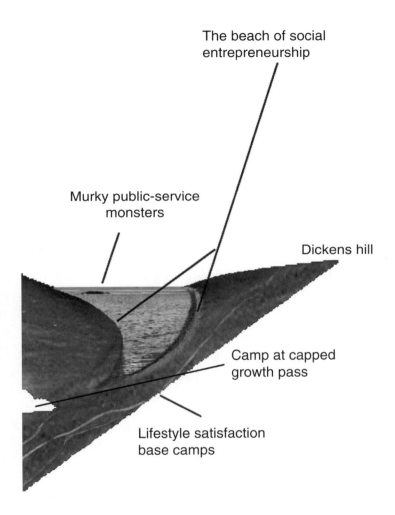

The beach of social entrepreneurship

Murky public-service monsters

Dickens hill

Camp at capped growth pass

Lifestyle satisfaction base camps

the multi-skilled middle management innovation drumlin on the

BOOSTING FACTORS • FACTORS THAT STOP INNOVATION • A SUMMARY OF LESSONS LEARNT FROM KVT • RECOMBINING KNOWLEDGE AND LEARNING PROVOKES INSPIRATION • **SOME CONCLUSIONS AND SUMMING UP** • CHOOSING POSSIBLE TECHNOLOGIES • CALCULATE YOUR BENEFIT • LARGER ORGANIZATIONS

12   119

Management). Being able to assemble and mine data sets leads us logically on to Decision Making, which in turn overlaps with Chance Discovery and other Innovation/Business Intelligence areas (reaching an extreme in BPR). Clearly at this stage, security aspects as well as legal and ethical issues are also important topics for the student. However, a large part of Information Systems involves being able to present accumulated information in such a way that it is understandable (i.e. learnable) and in context (i.e. within both a human/pedagogical and a business rules framework). Clearly in external facing and business contexts this encompasses e-commerce, HCI and usability. But since we are talking about IT-facilitated communication and learning then obviously more can be done, e.g. e-learning, games ('serious games') and mobile/wireless platforms ('just-in-time' learning). Thus one may pose the question; what technology to use? This question is pursued in more detail in Chapter 12, section 12.4, however here I just take a moment to consider that the technology does not exist, or not yet.

In Figure 12.2 I present SW-theory. SW does not stand for South West, but rather stands for time wasters (W) and time savers (S). In this example the Internet is taken to exemplify TCP/IP-based information sharing systems. The Internet started in the late 1960s and 1970s as a military application then increasingly an academic area. As such it was SW neutral, neither wasting nor saving the users' time. After 1994 and the advent of the WWW protocols the Internet started to take off, and the early drivers were pornography and gambling. I call these time wasters and the curve dips accordingly to the W. It took a long time for time savers like Amazon (started online trading in July 1995) and then – some years later – Internet banking, to reverse this trend and move the curve S-wards. During this time much technology was developed. However the curve dips W-wards again after 2004 (the founding of Facebook) as social sites, and also games became predominant. But my first point is that the technology became much more sophisticated too – HTML and Flash being largely dropped in favour of e.g. Ruby and Ajax. My second point is that the technology has evolved, implying that you can't jump to technical sophistication without points on the way, just as proto-chimps could not become *Homo sapiens* without evolving through intermediate – e.g. *Ardipithecus* – forms: The intermediates are necessary.

Figure 12.2 implies that the Internet is ready for a big swing to the S. What could this be? For example, I could imagine using Google Maps to zoom in on my street, right click on the lamp-post outside and choose from the menu 'report light to the local council as defective'. That would be a great time-saver, but it would need a novel combination of GIS, server programming and perhaps Games Technology (imagine navigating the Internet with a Wii/wiimote!) and unfortunately the technology is simply not developed yet. Similarly it may simply be that the technology needed to drive your Business-oriented Information System is not yet available, and you will have to recognize this and prune your ambitions back to the possible (in Google Maps click on a house to phone the

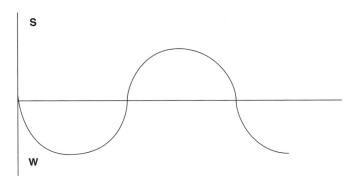

Figure 12.2 **The development of time saving (S) and time wasting (W) trends on the Internet with progressing time.**

occupant?). An overview of the abstract concepts, principles and some existing technologies needed to build your IT-driven knowledge management system, are given in Chapter 13.

12.4 Concepts around IT-driven knowledge management systems

We have seen that Information Systems aims to lower entropy in I-Space (Figure 2.3). The implications for this at an individual level, to some extent, depend on the individual's starting point on the Social Learning Cycle (Figure 2.2). New staff, for example, are beginners in the organization and may wish to locate business rules, handbooks and procedures. For this, static IT systems like MS-Sharepoint may be useful, although in an SME context some may plump for free services like Scribd.

This introduction for staff – flow diagrams and so on – can be considered to be part of Phase1 (scanning) of the SLC and involves N-learning (Chapter 11, section 11.2). In this respect, issues relevant to learning and e-learning have been touched upon in the e-learning case study (Chapter 2, section 2.4), furthermore, Chapter 11, section 11.4 has briefly mentioned double-loop learning (Argyris & Schön, 1974) and summarized the Dreyfus Model of Skills Acquisition (Dreyfus & Dreyfus, 1986). A book is an exceptionally good piece of hardware. Book technology has been debugged for hundreds of years and, although they still need a better 'search' mechanism, they represent a peak of perfection. An e-learning solution has therefore to be much better than a book-based solution if it is to succeed, including in a business environment: To put it bluntly, why make e-learning, if a book is better? As pointed out before, e-learning should concentrate on S-learning (Chapter 11, section 11.2). One example of how this can be done is shown in Case 10:

When and where can new technology be introduced?

Books are real competition to IT-driven learning systems, and books 'normally' win. So a project group of MSc students at the IT University of Copenhagen simply avoided competition from books by choosing a target group for their system that consisted of people who had great difficulty in reading (i.e. analphabetic and dyslectic persons) but who wanted to pass the high-level driving test to become taxi drivers etc. Their Flash-based solution was a great success since it did not rely on – or compete with – text at all, and it was superior to static graphical illustrations such as conventional slides and so on.

This is what Edward DeBono means by 'sur/petition' (DeBono, 1996), creating new markets instead of competing on existing markets.

The delivery of e-learning is probably best as a mixture of methods, balancing the disadvantages of Internet with the disadvantages of standalone programming. From Table 11.2 we can gather that focus can be achieved by defining where the learner is now, and what level they should achieve (e.g. from novice to advanced beginner) whereas the very highest levels are probably not achievable with e-learning. Relating back to S-learning it can be summarized that learning can be achieved as a series of 'ah-ha' experiences, where each is followed by a period of reflection and repetition involving trial and error. Gardner's theory (Gardner, 1983) that different individuals have different strengths warns that multimedia-based approaches may not be able to teach all types of people and subjects, especially the very practically oriented (plumbing etc.). A review of this enormous body of work can be found in standard text books (e.g. Ozmon & Craver, 2003).

The theories relating to all phases of the Social Learning Cycle (as it impacts on the content of IT-driven Knowledge Management systems) have been reviewed and, upon reflection, appear to overlap significantly or at least have common themes:

1. Diversity Innovation (Chapter 3) puts much emphasis on open channels enabling people with unlike knowledge to 'mutually inspire' each other.
2. Weak ties theory (Chapter 11, section 11.1) again states that sources of information that are not part of an individual's immediate circle are disproportionately more important.
3. S-learning (Chapter 11, section 11.3) describes the flash of understanding, the 'ah-ha experience' when the pieces fall into place.

Plus, of course the system finally implemented should not only archive but share knowledge between nodes in the Knowledge Valley (Chapter 6), present these with relatively seamless semantic interoperability so as to create innovation and thus drive the enterprise in question in an entrepreneurial direction, by helping create newer and better value chains (Chapter 4).[1]

These underpinning theoretical considerations do not help much with a process of actually constructing an information-sharing system, although some technologies (virtual reality, XML etc.) have been alluded to in Chapter 2, section 2.4, but again please do not get bogged down in technicalities, indeed the increasing use of Ruby/Rails or Python flavours like Django in web development and cloud-based services like gCloud or Salesforce are making technical database details such as database type (Oracle, mySQL, Access etc.) increasingly irrelevant.

Those interested in developing systems of mass collaboration (i.e. a 'we-think' or 'The Wisdom of Crowds' type approaches may also profit by reading the original works (Leadbeater, 2009 and Surowiecki, 2005, respectively). The IT technology equivalent of the 'wisdom of crowds' concept may well be multi-agent system (for a recent review, see Shoham & Leyton-Brown, 2008) which also utilizes the concept that one agent can be wrong, but lots together have a tendency to be right. Certainly the IT systems will contain Web 2.0 and User Generated Content e.g. microblogging and other techniques of 'social computing' (see e.g. Levine & Locke, 2009; Raymond, 2001; Safko & Brake, 2009), like Jive, Salesforce Chatter or Yammer. Horton (2000) and many subsequent authors have published works and recommendations on 'learning' implementations.

Much Knowledge Management may be simple; you may be faced with a problem that someone else has already solved, thus it appears reasonable to try to adopt a knowledge sharing approach so as to raise efficiency, lower response times and avoid splintering – i.e. generally lowering the transaction costs for communication. Grouping users according to their place on the Social Learning Cycle (above) already leads us to consider some aspects of web design, like doorway pages, with vertical or horizontal entry (for more on these concepts, see Mellor, 2003b, chapter 11) and indeed many aims and characteristics are similar to e-business. As such, some common concepts like asset specificity can be borrowed from e-commerce; indeed Kelly (1998) suggests that e-commerce possesses four attributes:

- exchange of digitalized information between parties
- it is technology enabled
- it is technology mediated
- it includes supporting activities that are intra- and inter-organizational.

And all of these four attributes appear relevant to the IT systems that may be used for electronic Knowledge Management systems. Rayport and Sviokla (1995) gave rise to the concept that products (and, indeed companies) move in a virtual

---

[1] An IT developer looking at this list plus e.g. streaming media, SMS facilities for Just-In-Time knowledge etc. often say; 'crikey, this is complicated I'm bound to get this wrong' and thus they plump for an open-source systems, so at least if they make a sub-optimal system they can change, avoiding being locked into a suboptimal system due to having high upfront investment costs!

BOOSTING FACTORS • FACTORS THAT STOP INNOVATION • A SUMMARY OF LESSONS LEARNT FROM KVT • RECOMBINING KNOWLEDGE AND LEARNING PROVOKES INSPIRATION • **SOME CONCLUSIONS AND SUMMING UP** • CHOOSING POSSIBLE TECHNOLOGIES • CALCULATE YOUR BENEFIT • LARGER ORGANIZATIONS

12   123

space (marketspace instead of marketplace). This was refined by Angerhahn (1997) in the publication '*The ICDT model; towards a taxonomy of Internet-related business strategies*'. Those wanting a readily understandable review may see Leong (1998). ICDT stands for: virtual Information space, virtual Communication space, virtual Distribution space and virtual Transaction space. A company must be established in all four virtual spaces before it can be said to be established in the virtual marketspace. This being said, the entry into all four spaces is not normally simultaneous, but rather an evolution, typically starting in the information space. ICDT is normally depicted as four extra (virtual) spaces surrounding the traditional market place thus (Figure 12.3):

Figure 12.3 **Review of the ICDT view of e-commerce, the four virtual spaces.**

In the ICDT model, the abbreviations stand for:

- VIS stands for Virtual Information Space. In B2C e-commerce this is often the space that companies inhabit first. At its most primitive it is used as a 'virtual billboard' where companies relatively cheaply can advertise and inform about themselves and their products/services.
- VCS stands for Virtual Communication Space. In VIS communication is overwhelmingly one way, from the company to the customer. In VCS space companies use new channels to enter into two-way relationships and exchanges of ideas with their customers, perhaps even enabling cross-customer contact. Technically, the possibilities include e-mail, chat rooms, bulletin board systems etc.
- VDS stands for Virtual Distribution Space and represents a new digital distribution channel or network. Clearly not all products can be distributed virtually (furniture etc.), but VDS may still be useful in distributing help programs, support and extra service (e.g. how to assemble the furniture).
- VTS stands for Virtual Transaction Space. This space focuses on business-related transactions, and not only customer-facing (payment gateway etc.) transactions, but also transactions in the enabling process, e.g. supply chain management.

Problems with ICDT include that it totally lacks any kind of quantitative aspect, and indeed the representation of the four virtual spaces as being equally important may be misleading for any specific company or analysis. For the type of IT-systems under discussion, VTS may well be irrelevant in some enterprises.

Furthermore information is only forward-looking in the value system, ignoring possibilities or changes that innovations may cause in the value chain. Nonetheless we may be able to borrow some general principles (see e.g. Mellor, 2005a) from e-commerce for our purposes (Table 12.2).

Again to borrow a concept from e-commerce, driving people to a site where they do not convert into customers is pointless. In Business-oriented Information Systems the lesson is that the system must be so interesting (essential?) that people want to go there (i.e. traffic appears). Beyond roll-out, trying to boost traffic using gimmicks or glib snippets (I refer to the foreword concerning the inability of journalists to promote Diversity Innovation) is ultimately a waste of time.

Table 12.2 **Summary of some of the better and less well-known findings resulting from Knowledge Valley Theory as related to adoption of e-commerce principles to IT-driven Knowledge Management systems.**

	'Common knowledge'	New (or at least less common) knowledge
Virtual Communication Space	Group dynamics help learning	Group dynamics must be carefully planned before group chat rooms etc. are opened, in fact open bulletin board systems (BBS, blogs etc.) first explode in chaos before becoming catatonic.
Virtual Communication Space	Innovation is 'good' and leaders should be committed to open information gateways.	It is the dominant consensus group (in practice, the middle management) in existing organizations in mature markets are over-proportionally active in defending their 'realm' against innovation.
Virtual Information Space	Updating separate web sites and print media is very work intensive.	Synchronize the internal intranet and the public Internet website so the staff and customers work from the same and updated catalogue.
Virtual Information Space	Simple searches are often insufficient because context is missing.	It is not possible to search in Google or other general Internet search engines for 'toothpaste' while specifying that the results returned should be of interest to those in a particular income bracket, with false teeth and living in a particular area.
Virtual Distribution Space	The adoption of e-commerce is more successful where Internet competencies are closely related to the company's core competencies.	Organizations whose competencies include Knowledge Management and IT are probably going to be examples of best practice.
Use of IT in Knowledge Management	IT systems help a little, but not much, often due to confusion between KM systems and static document archives.	'e-learning' should always be aimed at the 'lowest common denominator', e-learning helps those who may otherwise drop out, but will rarely help 'super-users'.

Standard Business Information Systems are often relatively simple intranets with searchable document repositories. However a central justification of Business Information Systems is that they should recombine knowledge – both tacit and explicit – to promote innovation which in turn promotes the creation of new value chains, a target that mere intranets with searchable document repositories cannot achieve. In order to be useful tools for knowledge management and push the organization in entrepreneurial directions, they need to impart knowledge, strengthen networks and encourage both learning and mutual inspiration.

A conceptual model for knowledge sharing in SMEs was presented in Figure 2.4. This can be expanded upon by recombining the factors touched upon in this section. From these it can be seen that a multi-layered model of Business-oriented Information Systems aligned with core competencies can be envisaged. In this model (Figure 12.3, below) we look again at Figure 1.1, the interlinked – in a Venn diagram sense – areas of Knowledge Management, Entrepreneurship and Innovation. To briefly reiterate, this juxtaposition points out that Knowledge Management should provoke Innovation (including in a 'mutual inspiration' sense) in an entrepreneurial fashion to benefit the enterprise, where the enterprise involved can be commercial or non-profit, etc. The point is to create better ways of doing things – new value chains – as explained in Figure 4.1.

The next layer is pedagogy, consisting of understandable, learnable (S-learnable?) explanations in context and indeed how to best do this is still the focus of considerable research, but at least the plethora of textbooks on e.g. Entrepreneurship would indicate that most of these topics are principally learnable. However by no means everything is communicated by pedagogical methods, so the Knowledge Management, Entrepreneurship and Innovation constellation is not a subset of pedagogical considerations.

To interface with an electronic system, an e-learning layer may be added. As mentioned previously, much e-learning (e.g. that concerning children and early learning) lies outside the topic of this book, but some techniques of adult e-learning could be adapted.

Clearly there are also areas where an e-learning middle layer to the electronic (IT-driven) system is not appropriate; these may be e.g. data mining or specialized queries on warehoused data. So in the model (Figure 12.3) the e-learning layer does not extend completely 'across the board'. Similarly the borders are not uniformly permeable as special stakeholders, expert subject specialists and so on may arise in specific areas in the context of altruistic mentors as mentioned in Chapter 2, section 2.2. Such philanthropists (if they exist in that enterprise) will form direct channels or conduits through the model.

The lower layer, the computer-mediated interface with the user, could profitably borrow many concepts from e-commerce systems (Figure 12.4). As explained above, the ICDT model is particularly useful. VIS could for example include business rules and factual information of a more static nature. VCS could contain

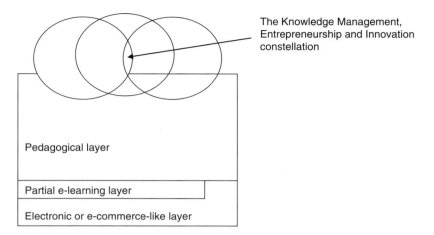

The Knowledge Management, Entrepreneurship and Innovation constellation

Pedagogical layer

Partial e-learning layer

Electronic or e-commerce-like layer

Figure 12.4 **Conceptual layers of a Knowledge Management electronic system for a learning and knowledge sharing environment.**

Table 12.3 **Some similarities in content categories between the Information Systems, ICDT and SECI models.**

IS	ICDT category	SECI category
Signalling	VCS	Externalization
Content	VIS	Socialization
Social	VDS & VTS	Socialization
Interaction	VDS & VTS	Combination & Internalization

alerts (one-to-many communication) or blogs and so on. VDS may contain e.g. product information while VTS could be smarter ways of streamlining the business processes (CRM, ERP, etc.).

The Information Systems technologies to be investigated comprise four broad categories: Signaling, Content, Social and Interaction (see Figure 2.4 and Chapter 2, section 2.5). These categories map to some extent to those in the ICDT (Figure 12.1) and SECI (Figure 2.1) models as given in Table 12.3.

Clearly innovation can also be applied to IT-driven systems too, certainly combining telephony (and mobile technology) and TCP/IP may result in novel and potentially useful combinations. However the concrete solution implemented will hardly be generic. One may argue from considerations around information gatekeeping that a universal feature will be in enabling users to by-pass formalities. However this and other security issues will be determined by the type of data stored; in some industry branches (e.g. the banking/finance industry) inappropriate use will be a very important item on the agenda. In other sectors e.g. health and pharmaceuticals, regulatory compliance may be uttermost, especially as unforeseen legislation may hit at almost any time.

BOOSTING FACTORS · FACTORS THAT STOP INNOVATION · A SUMMARY OF LESSONS LEARNT FROM KVT · RECOMBINING KNOWLEDGE AND LEARNING PROVOKES INSPIRATION · **SOME CONCLUSIONS AND SUMMING UP** · CHOOSING POSSIBLE TECHNOLOGIES · CALCULATE YOUR BENEFIT · LARGER ORGANIZATIONS

12   127

13   choosing possible technologies

Web 2 technologies are powerful and widely applicable. For example, a Funambol server – not even necessarily on stage – would enable musicians to send their performances direct and in real time to the mobile phones of their fans all over the world. But exactly how the business model for this disruptive technology would work is quite a different matter.

So once again we see that technology is not a solution in itself – it requires a clear understanding of the issues involved and – especially in an SME context – a concerted effort on the part of management to define their challenges and objectives. Only then can a decision be made if and how technology can help be a part of the solution. That being so, it must be underlined that this chapter is no way prescriptive; what works for you depends on your people, your context, your environment and your business.

That said, there are common concepts to be taken into account, the major being interoperability (the ability of different systems to communicate with each other and reuse existing information assets). Web Ontology Language (OWL) is often quoted in this respect. Well-documented examples of the use of OWL are national initiatives like Deutschland Online and FinnONTO (Finland) and trans-national initiatives like SemanticGOV (Figure 13.1).

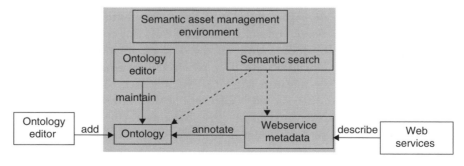

Figure 13.1   **Semantic interoperability, a theoretical OWL architecture.**

13.1   Soft issues

As seen from Chapters 8 to 10 some of the innovation-boosting and innovation-preventing factors in an organization are in areas not immediately amenable to impact by IT systems. These include e.g. hiring multi-specialists in middle management and the formation of task forces, which are HR/leadership decisions.

Nevertheless an intranet as the basic form of corporate communication is probably unavoidable, and one should try to make the best out of it. Company intranet pages should start by displaying basic information – perhaps in FAQs (Frequently Asked Questions) form explaining 'how to' type information; how to book a room, claim expenses, find a pen or perform some other basic task. There should also be a 'who's who' and indeed the intranet should display photos of all staff and these could furthermore have a business network style (e.g. linkedin.com, spoke.com or xing.com) style self-description. In principle there could be an indicator on the page indicating if the person is a multi-specialist (although the deeper meaning of this may be lost on many), and it may display who this person is mentoring or is mentored by, if they have a blog, etc. An expert-finding system (e.g. askmecorp.com) is probably overkill in a typical SME where a 'social Ethernet' of mouth-to-mouth contacts will suffice, although one could consider such a system in larger organizations. There could be other indicators of popularity on individuals' personal intranet pages and such measures may reduce 'leadership rift' (Chapter 9) by making leaders and executives more approachable. As such these pages may represent the direct channels or conduits through the e-learning layer as shown in Figure 12.3.

Previously the effect of exclusion zones around very close connections was seen (Chapter 10, section 10.6). Thus a corporate intranet would not be expected to have a dating section – indeed that could readily be frowned upon. Conversely it may have an exchange (buy and sell) section so employees really may meet those outside their immediate work circle. Similarly with task forces, although the formation of truly autonomous task forces should be discouraged (see Chapter 10, section 10.7), an annual reunion of members of disbanded task forces may well be beneficial as those ties may with time have become Granovetrian 'weak ties' (see Chapter 11, section 11.1).

Similarly, seniors and retired staff may be given paid (or indeed unpaid) opportunities via an extranet or other form of telecommuting-like arrangement; one could expand this to e.g. helping mentoring new staff and so on, thus minimizing the 'Lost Knowledge' phenomenon (Chapter 9).

13.2   Systems construction – principles for SMEs

We will not go into the technical basis of web 2.0 technologies (XML, SOAP, WSDL and UDDI) nor programming languages like the Go programming language, or C++, Android/Java, Django (Python on Rails), Ruby (on Rails or not), nor specific construction software such as Dreamweaver, XMetaL, ConText or Visual InterDev and so on, because these are more Computer Science topics. Fortunately included in our take-home message is that again we are fortunate in that the presence and availability of lightweight programming techniques and tools (e.g. Yahoo Pipes) and that means that one does not have to be highly qualified to become (or function as) a developer. Another new concept is the reuse of prototypes. Prototypes (cars, planes etc.) are traditionally discarded before production, but Agile Development methods concentrate on retrieving as much as possible from software prototypes. The central concept is that an 'agile' continually evolving mashup – especially if it is cloud-based – is appropriate for rapidly developing organizations that wish to avoid deadly legacy systems. This is a cheap solution, with a low IT footprint in the organization and – as pointed out in Chapter 12 (Table 12.1) 'Early mistakes... may haunt you for an inordinate time afterwards' so early large IT investments may no longer appear so enticing in the light of a nimble alternative that can be updated (or disposed of) at a moments notice.

It used to be said that a website was never finished. This 'old' adage is truer today than ever when not only the construction itself, but also the tools, applications, APIs and so on, are now in a state of 'continual beta'. The myth that gigantic IT systems can be built that does everything for everyone and forever, is well over. Hopefully the last example (probably the NHS IT system that as I write, is six years behind schedule and 24 million pounds over budget) has been seen. Fortunately exactly this chaotic and continually evolving landscape fits well the needs of SMEs and especially those that wish to progress from mice to gazelles (or elephants to gazelles). Software as a service (SaaS, see e.g. strikeiron.com) means that cash strapped SMEs do not need to make large investments in software, can upgrade when they want while cloud computing minimizes their legacy systems. They can use what they need and then discard it at will, adding new facets to their systems as they grow. Probably also – especially in an SME environment – one does not need to implement everything: in the real world, one should not be surprised if the Pareto Rule applies; 20% of what is available will satisfy 80% of all needs. Furthermore the edges between technologies are becoming blurred so choice of a particular functionality may well follow available resources, which change in a developmental fashion as the organization evolves and grows: For example, with work sharing in a particular environment one may wish to start with a free collaborative mashup – like Google Wave – then later progressing to a more secure widget system like e.g. Work Light (worklight.com) while for a similar function a large and more solvent organization may prefer an out-of-the-box solution like MS Groove similarly an organization may choose a free CRM like SugarCRM before they invest in e.g. MS Dynamics CRM, these again may usefully have links to other corporate services, typically the IT helpdesk, which in turn may be running a proprietary product like Hewlett Packard Open View or open source alternatives like Request Tracker or Summit Seven. Obviously slightly different flavours are also available – people on the move may appreciate the free munote mobile note-sharing application (munote.com) over e.g. MS OneNote. These could well be integrated into a software umbrella like Semantic Mediawiki. The point is that the flexibility allows rapid development according to external conditions and thus facilitates organizational response, resilience and ultimately growth.

13.4 Sectors and levels

Social Network Systems (SNS) are relatively easy to set up, have been piloted in larger organizations and have met with mixed success. For our use an SNS is insufficient for us, because in our scenario the employees are safe behind a secure firewall and are engaged in deriving information from corporate data, as well as customer-facing applications, B2B collaboration (see e.g. blueroads.com or PeopleSoft partner management), plus other trading and sourcing information, while learning and sharing the knowledge gained (see Figures 2.4 and 2.5) to create new value for the organization. Thus many more systems than just SNS and the transaction processing system have to be cobbled (mashed) together, but also contain the transaction processing system, because the Information System would ideally also include the addition of corporate data, Key Performance Indicators (KPIs) and an executive economic forecast (because cash-flow is so crucially important for SMEs) and report this as business intelligence (see e.g. businessobjects.com) and decision support (see Figures 2.1 and 2.2). Already now one can see that not everything is applicable to everyone in an organization: This gives rise to the concepts of tiered sectors.

In principle the tiers or levels in an organization are operational, managerial and executive. An SNS is clearly useful at an operational level (where it should be generating mutual inspiration) and at a managerial level where managers should be scanning for improvements as part of their duties as information gatekeepers. However SNS is of little value at executive level. Exactly the converse situation is true in the case of e.g. economic forecasting, where the information should probably be restricted to executive levels, and only interest the managerial level in terms of budgets. One should also consider small or specialist sectors in the organization; e-procurement, HR and complaints handling/refunds are three examples.

These functions are to be selected and mixed appropriately in a kind of 'Organizational IT Aggregator'. As an extension of the term CRM, I call this a KRM – Knowledge Relations Management – and it is a continually evolving set of functions impacting procedures, people, organizational structure and business processes. I should make the reader aware that other authors have a related taxonomy for concepts that are not dissimilar e.g. Knowledge Management Systems in Newell et al. (2009) and indeed some go as far as to label enterprises implementing Web 2.0 technologies as 'Enterprise 2.0' (McAfee, 2006). There will probably be a nomenclature shakeout at some point in the future.

In section 13.5 we will take a closer look at some specific functions.

13.5 Analysis – Preparing the ground

Obviously specialists in Information Systems realize the importance of carefully preparing the ground before embarking on a new project. Traditionally this involves a stakeholder analysis, cost estimates and project (and risk) management, which together result in a Project Initiation Document plus (preferably) a set of specifications, which are then considered for a go/no go decision by senior management.

Now, however, the Information Systems specialist is able to incorporate the insights provided by Knowledge Valley Theory and although this means arguing to senior management for the benefits, it does also for the first time give the practitioner a method of estimating not only costs, but the benefits too (see Part V and especially Chapter 14). Thus the Project Initiation Document, with its PERT and Gantt charts and so on, comes more to resemble a Business Plan aimed at convincing senior management or at least giving them a solid basis for a rational decision. This is to my mind an exciting and satisfying upgrading of the tasks confronting Information Systems specialists, arguing in an informed fashion for an IT-driven Knowledge Management system that affects the bottom line, influences business processes (let's go back and revisit Figure 1.1) and indeed is a kind of 'e-TQM', instead of being reactive the possibly uninformed (possibly abysmally misinformed!) management wish for an intranet.

This may seem like more work, but in fact the highly flexible nature of the continually evolving project to be undertaken will mean that rigid project management structures like Prince 2 could sensibly be discarded in favour of more lightweight tools like ITIL. Indeed Prince 2 may be overkill anyway for many SME environments.

The actual analysis will probably use pre-construction design principles and techniques that specialists in Information Systems are already equipped with. These include project management (Cadle & Yeats, 2008), SoA, UML and SSADM, whereby SSADM (a rather laborious and UK-specific methodology) is slowly becoming replaced by UML. Those considering Agile Development methods (see Chapter 13, section 13.2) will probably include DSDM. Specialists in Information Systems should be able to understand what technologies can do, but a detailed consideration of these tools goes far beyond the more humble aims of this book: They are considered to already be part of the readers 'Information Systems toolkit'.

13.6 Some software building bricks

In Chapter 13, section 13.2 the NHS was referred to as an example of the myth that gigantic IT systems can be built that does everything for everyone and forever. This is an important point as flexible implementation and evolution in an SME context is not Gargantuan (gigantic) but rather expressly Lilliputian. Characteristics of a good Information Systems specialist will include a lively and up-to-date knowledge of what is 'out there'. Obviously this can change rapidly, as indeed is the nature of Web 2.0. and many theoretically useful and interesting technologies like iPing (multi message broadcasting), mocospace (mobile advertising/SNS), bluepulse (mobile networking), brightkite (mobile video sharing), zyb (phone data backup), gruvr (event mapping), gypsii (mobile location sharing) and fon11(telephony through a web browser) may not even exist by the time you read this book – or indeed may have become the next Google. In this bewildering world some support does thankfully exist and resources for the Information Systems specialist are available on the web (e.g. the website of the Association for Information Systems, isworld.org).

Social Business Systems (SBS) are listed below, but not the better-known examples of social networking (SNS) services such as MySpace, Facebook, Flickr, Twitter, Friend Connect, Open Social, Platial, Tumbler or Topix, for the simple reason that employers are often uneasy seeing their employees spending their a large part of their working hours on the above-mentioned sites.

However we have discussed some Web 2.0 and other technologies in Chapter 2, section 2.4 and again in Chapter 12, section 12.4, so it may be useful to just get a collected overview. For the avoidance of doubt I will repeat that the systems mentioned here are just some examples and many others exist (interested readers can undoubtedly find more on the web); inclusion here is by no means a recommendation and exclusions are my ignorant omissions, with no slight intended. On the bright side, much of this technology is surprisingly simple to implement, as well as being effective and readers will find examples in the appendices. For example, imagine finding a document in your repository that is written in incomprehensible 'bureaucratese' (and this extends to software conceptions and architecture, for example software like MS Sharepoint is often cynically referred to as 'Graveyard'). However in our innovative case imagine that the author biographical data actually contains a link. So using <callto: > code and a Skype address, you will be able to click to a video link with the author and ask them what they actually mean (or would have liked to write ... or other penetrating question). In the following some examples of useful technologies that could be used in a simple Information Systems context (see e.g. Figure 2.4) are illustrated. The interested reader will have no difficulty in finding further examples, or detailed explanation of these examples, on the web. For convenience the list is divided into two parts, those dealing with specific application areas (Table 13.1), followed by those which relate more to an organizations functional area as given in Table 13.2.

Table 13.1 **Possible software solutions for application areas.**

Application Area	Examples	Comments
CRM, ERP and other collaborative planning software	Sugar Hipergate Compiere SAP Vtiger Open Bravo	There is a bewilderingly wide offering that has exploded since Lotus Notes and IBM WebSphere.
Databases	Cloud-based services replacing dedicated servers and apps e.g. Oracle mySQL and MS-Access	See e.g. Salesforce.com, gCloud and elastic compute cloud (Amazon)
Decision-making/concept management and Business Intelligence tools:	NVIVO Decision Explorer Frontier Analyst Cognos Hyperion	Contrast 'Clarity' or Open Workbench, tools for project management.
Images	Streaming video/media (e.g. podcasting) youTube Ajax Skype video conferencing	Skype offers what is basically free video-conferencing, for SMEs an attractive alternative to e.g. Polycom HDX teleconferencing.
Languages/translation	Babel Fish Google Language Tools Systran Avalon for Language Voice synthesis (Phraselator etc.)	Machine translation is now surprisingly good. Some are available with marionettes for sign language. Speech synthesis plug-ins are available that read text (e.g. on websites or in emails) aloud.
Social computing/User Generated Content	blogs/microblogging Mashups (Pipes etc.). Wikis	Contemporary equivalents of (live) chat rooms – encourages participation
Signalling	Email/instant messaging MS-OneNote RSS Phone (Callto) links/VoIP SMS	Cutting response time either personalized or one-to-many
Spatial	Google Maps Trimble Nav MapInfo GIS/GPS Frappr	Geographical is another obvious way of sorting data.
Social Business Systems	Salesforce Chatter Yammer Jive SBS	Many-to-many socialization

Continued

GENERAL INTRODUCTION • INTRODUCTION TO KNOWLEDGE MANAGEMENT • INTRODUCTION TO INNOVATION • INTRODUCTION TO ENTREPRENEURSHIP • INTRODUCTION TO SMES • CONSTRUCTING KNOWLEDGE VALLEY • MANAGING FORMAL KNOWLEDGE • USING KVT TO IDENTIFY INNOVATION

Table 13.1 **Continued**

Application Area	Examples	Comments
Virtual reality (3D)	SimCity/Open Sim Second Life Wonder World O3D	Useful for many-to-many cooperation at a distance. And fun too!
Web-based document management	Xoops Joomla Drupal Moodle Mahara	I have excluded purely educational software like Blackboard and WebCT and bundled offerings like Lotus Quickr.
File sharing	Scribd Google Docs MS-Sharepoint/Groove BitTorrent (video)	In an SME context a simple shared drive may be sufficient.

Table 13.2. **Possible software solutions for organizational/functional sectors.**

Functional Sector	Primary	Secondary
Executive	Business performance management (e.g. prophix.com) and business analytics (e.g. capterra.com)	Further integration with data mining (e.g. gViz or Wizsoft.com)
HR	Solutions like People-trak.com but also tracking employee benefits e.g. iemployee.com	Recruitment e.g. Monster.com, salary.com and jobcentral.com
Financial	Accounting (claritysystems.com) or transactions sales/invoicing (e.g. Oanda, Peachtree, etc)	Conversions like currency (xe.com) or other measurements (metric-conversions.org)
e-procurement	Connections to preferred suppliers e.g. fotolia.com, crowdspring.com or stamps.com	Also ad hoc procurement, like madbird or swoopo, but note that this is not supply chain management (SCM, sometimes known as 'e-supply').
Cash flow	Financial projections e.g. extensity.com (infor.com) or cybershift.com	Handling expenses claims e.g. concur.com
Customer complaints	A web front end like Qitconsulting.com or Qms-software.com	The only limits are your imagination e.g. voice-to-text tools like Nuance Dragon or Tellme.com

Please note that many more integrations are possible, e.g. with the mail server and other software. However the above is not a recipe book. Every implementation will be subtly (or radically) different because every SME exists in its own unique context, somewhere along its own unique developmental path.

GENERAL   INTRODUCTION   •   INTRODUCTION   TO   KNOWLEDGE   MANAGEMENT   •
O INNOVATION • INTRODUCTION TO ENTREPRENEURSHIP • INTRODUCTION
RUCTING KNOWLEDGE VALLEY • MANAGING FORMAL KNOWLEDGE • USING
KVT TO IDENTIFY INNOVATION BOOSTING FACTORS • FACTORS THAT STOP INNOVATION
• A SUMMARY OF LESSONS LEARNT FROM KVT. • RECOMBINING KNOWLEDGE AND
LEARNING PROVOKES INSPIRATION. • SOME CONCLUSIONS AND SUMMING UP • CHOOSING
POSSIBLE TECHNOLOGIES • CALCULATE YOUR BENEFIT • LARGER ORGANIZATIONS

Part V the practitioner view

Context and aims

In Part I we established a common baseline by agreeing on which parts of what topics are relevant for ours. It was a skimming exercise because the parts (Knowledge Management, Business Innovation, Entrepreneurship and Information Systems) are each for themselves a lifetimes study – we have to grab what we can.

In Part II we erected a mathematical and quite abstract theory, called Knowledge Valley Theory, from first principles.

In Part III we tested what we had got by a fairly clear modelling; it told us some new truths and confirmed a lot of 'truths' that old hands know – albeit that they knew it without knowing why.

In Part IV we saw some applications – what technology can be used where or in what situation. Obviously a 'killer' technology can appear at any time and re-write the whole script, but what was described as state-of-the-art and successful innovations tend not to be several steps ahead (i.e. not 'bleeding edge') but tend rather to be incremental, so perhaps this will not change too much during the lifetime of this book.

But the laws of mercantile activity are immutable: Someone will ask 'how much does it cost' and 'what is my benefit in monetary terms'? The cost will change as value chains in the hardware and software industries become more efficient (new value chains ... the whole point of this book) and software prices plummet. But how much is the benefit is a question that all canny consultants avoid. The next Chapter, however, bravely tries to put financial values on this, as well as expanding the model to larger entities, beyond SMEs.

At the end of this chapter the reader should be able to estimate with reasonable precision the financial benefits an organization may accrue as a result of implementing 'best practice' Information Systems.

14 calculate your benefit

CTION TO INNOVATION • INTRODUCTION TO ENTREPRENEURSHIP • INTRODUCTION
• CONSTRUCTING KNOWLEDGE VALLEY • MANAGING FORMAL KNOWLEDGE • USING
KVT TO IDENTIFY INNOVATION BOOSTING FACTORS • FACTORS THAT STOP INNOVATION
• A SUMMARY OF LESSONS LEARNT FROM KVT • RECOMBINING KNOWLEDGE AND
LEARNING PROVOKES INSPIRATION • SOME CONCLUSIONS AND SUMMING UP • CHOOSING
POSSIBLE TECHNOLOGIES • CALCULATE YOUR BENEFIT • LARGER ORGANIZATIONS

Clearly after reading the foregoing chapters you will be asking yourselves various questions. These will all assume (the 'killer assumption') that Knowledge Valley Theory is not only correct and applicable in a practical sense, but will then quickly go on to include various themes around 'how can I benefit'. This generic question quickly reveals itself to be composed of a set of sub-questions, like:

- Where am I in the Knowledge Valley?
- If I am on the 'wrong side', then how deep are the depths (of the Tarn) for me?
- Can I get through these depths and, if so, what rewards are there on the other side?

In asking these questions, the bad news is that the general and generic picture painted in the previous chapters is unlikely to me of much specific use for your particular company. The good news is that it can be applied, but it needs some more input from you (well, quite a lot more, actually).

As a start, the comparison data for some of the figures are detailed below in Table 14.1.

Table 14.1 **An overview of the data used in preparing figures 6.10, 6.13, 6.14 and 12.2. Financial values in British pounds (2008).**

Percent use of innovation	Average wage	Profit per employee	Income per worker	Minimum annual turnover
0	20000	13014	33014	8253500
10	20000	11447	31447	7861750
20	20000	9640	29640	7410000
30	18000	8194	26194	6548500
40	19000	7240	26240	6560000
50	20000	9399	29399	7349750
60	21000	14460	35460	8865000
70	25000	20485	45485	11371250
80	30000	26510	56510	14127500
90	35000	33740	68740	17185000
100	40000	40006	80006	20001500

So let's get going: Using Table 14.1 you will be able to prepare a similar table pertaining to where your company is in your branch. Table 14.1 – and the figures derived from it – are highly generic and likely to apply to any average SME struggling along in any European country in any not-particularly-profitable branch of any industry (normally a service industry). However average companies almost never exist in real life. Thus the factors need to be modified for each individual case. Here is a rough checklist of what you need to do:

1. First you need to modify the absolute height of the earnings. These are extremely variable between branches of industry – everybody knows that earning levels are different in different service branches, and if you don't believe me, then compare average personal income in two different branches like catering and hedge fund management, on a per-employee basis. The variation is quite significant (if not astounding).

2. Secondly you should use your branch knowledge to try and identify the end points of the innovation scale; which companies in your industry are the most Dickensian and which are the most innovative? At this point it is prudent to remember that these may not be 0% and 100% on the scale – for example hardly a decade ago there was no appreciable difference between those organizations providing personnel involved in cleaning office buildings, but today it is actually a finely tuned and highly competitive area using state-of-the-art time management techniques. Perhaps where you are (in the business universe) has not yet been subject to innovative focus. However, if it has, and continues to be (i.e. not everyone is through the tarn yet) then insider branch knowledge will not only identify these extreme cases, but will also indicate average wage and other factors like profit and income per worker in them, because these can be calculated back from annual records where e.g. annual turnover should be publicly available for Companies House or published returns.

3. Having done this you will thirdly have to adjust for company size (i.e. number of employees) using your best judgement; clearly it is risky comparing a company of 100 employees with one of 200 employees.

4. Fourthly a judicious choice has to be made about where your organization lies between the theoretical (and indeed invisible) end-points on the innovation scale of 0–100%. This needs to be weighed up in sober judgement, weighing innovative potentials against place in hierarchical structures. This is indeed only guestimable – and then only after years of working in that organization with a critical eye for which of your peers, superiors and subordinates contribute to the overall innovative potential, weighted by their ability to do so (information gatekeeping, etc).

5. Finally, having identified 3 or 4 points on your branches J-curve, the depth of the Tarn can be estimated. Obviously it is useful if a near competitor has just tried to wade through the Tarn, a few Christmas drinks with staff

from other companies should extract the information needed about decline in industrial strength, turnover and downsizing during the watery tour. However for my taste this smacks a bit too much of industrial espionage and I must repeat that with even only a handful of points, the J-curve can be calculated without resorting to shady tactics, no matter how enjoyable these may be. The point about being able to calculate the shape of the J-curve has been strenuously underlined before, in Chapter 6, section 6.2 and Chapter 8 and thus the only decision left is should the curve be similar to the generic curve shown (Figures 6.13–6.15) or Cartesian or Fibonacci? The choice is up to you, because you are the local expert with insight into your special branch of industry.

Using this checklist the generic may become the particular. If anyone would like to seriously apply this to their organization, then please get in touch because I would seriously like to hear from you.

15 larger organizations

CTION TO INNOVATION • INTRODUCTION TO ENTREPRENEURSHIP • INTRODUCTION CONSTRUCTING KNOWLEDGE VALLEY • MANAGING FORMAL KNOWLEDGE • USING KVT TO IDENTIFY INNOVATION BOOSTING FACTORS • FACTORS THAT STOP INNOVATION • A SUMMARY OF LESSONS LEARNT FROM KVT. • RECOMBINING KNOWLEDGE AND LEARNING PROVOKES INSPIRATION. • SOME CONCLUSIONS AND SUMMING UP • CHOOSING POSSIBLE TECHNOLOGIES • CALCULATE YOUR BENEFIT • LARGER ORGANIZATIONS

In this book some elementary mathematical concepts have been applied to innovation and knowledge management in smallish organizations. This begs the question; can the same principles be applied to larger organizations? SMEs grow, the supposition (see e.g. Mellor, 2008) being that they grow to a size greater than 250 employees and especially gazelles displace old competitors and lead to evolution and progress in industrial sectors, or indeed replacing industrial sectors (e.g. Microsoft and similar companies were responsible not only for making computers ubiquitous as an office tool, but also for major transformations in the publishing and communications sectors, even ingrained skills like map-reading are becoming rare as more individuals use GIS/GPS-based devices). Therefore, one may conclude, that modelling innovation in larger organizations is of fundamental importance. Unfortunately it is not so easy; a small business is not a small large business and vice versa.

The limits are:

1. **Technological:** Modelling KVT to an employee number of 200 stretches the limit of today's computing power. A number over 250 needs more processing capacity than is available.

2. **Economic:** In KVT, the axes can be labelled in actual monetary value because in small businesses the labour of each person can be calculated and their labour directly affects financial performance ('the bottom line'). This is not the case in large organizations where expensive functions may well be unrelated to any kind of direct productivity. Indeed the capital that a large organization possesses may consist of shares in other organizations, so overall profitability is partly determined by workers quite outside the reach of KVT initiatives (especially if these are 'gilt-edged' securities). Conversely, as stated in Chapter 10, section 10.5, large organizations may use corporate entrepreneurship ('intrapreneurship') to spin-out those innovations which the parent company cannot properly lever, so in that case the parent organizations capital may consist of shares in organizations using KVT-like initiatives.

3. **Organizational:** Any improvements made need to be quantified, but in large organizations the accounting methods are ill suited and the amounts to be credited to knowledge techniques are too fine grained to be caught and recognized, especially if they run for several years (i.e. over several accounting periods) and/or after an initial lag phase.
4. **Developmental:** Can KVT and associated techniques help large organizations? The credit crunch of 2008–09 saw various governments bailing out large organizations with hundreds of billions of pounds. The point is that for larger organizations KVT is not a valley, but probably something like a hull and this hull will rise and fall (and capsize?) on the groundswell of bull and bear markets to an extent that dwarfs other factors.

The above notwithstanding, we have seen general principles in Tables 12.1 and 12.2 and the practitioner will be able to understand that some of these are even more relevant to large organizations, e.g. information gate-keeping, especially between large divisions in a company. So now let us see what larger chunks of KVT can be applied to larger organizations.

15.1 Large organizations and KVT

Up to Chapter 8 the modelling used was based on the assumption that every node is connected to every node, and that all jumps between nodes are equally easy. In Chapters 8 and 9 perturbations like knowledge trails and exclusion zones were introduced and then again in Chapter 11 weak ties made the model more complicated again. Calculating where the Monte Carlo ball (see Chapter 8) may be at any one time in our computer simulation is thus very hard and even the introduction of weak ties exceeds the processing power available. Recall that in order to arrive at the results presented in Figure 8.3 the number of individuals was limited to 200 and a line of code had to be added to stop the balls going backwards (i.e. they were prevented from taking paths which would take them to nodes lying between 90° and 240° from the imaginary true line forward). So the number of degrees of freedom any node had, was reduced in the simple model presented from 199 to less than a quarter of that. These conditions were put in place in the model for SMEs using the argument was that everyone in an SME contributes fairly directly to the bottom line. We cannot simply use the same argument for large organizations, because in large organizations significant numbers of staff may be employed in activities which do not contribute – or at least not directly – to the bottom line. So in a large organization any one node may truly have an almost infinite number of degrees of freedom. At first sight this appears a reasonable assumption, because it implies that the transaction costs for communication increase, a common complaint in large organizations.

Let us try to visualize this: Try to imagine a cross between the Knowledge Valley and a pinball machine. Where the Monte Carlo ball hits a node, the node lights up. Previously the model worked by releasing a batch of Monte Carlo balls at the mouse position, resulting in a wave of light that would race down the valley. However now in a larger valley where nodes have more degrees of freedom the light waves will diffuse and race in any direction, up, across or whatever as nodes are hit by information – an illustration would be some kind of convection currents instigated by e.g. gossip and/or rumours, passing rapidly between nodes in any direction, not necessarily aligned to the best organizational or financial interests of the company (indeed it is well known that rumours etc. – perturbations in the DI net – are normally against the best interests of the organization and need to be handled firmly by top management in a timely fashion).

15.2   Chaos Theory

Indeed, one can begin to anticipate chaos. Figure 6.12 already hints that the system is intransitive, that is, it can stay stable in one state on one side, yet have reached a different equilibrium on the other. To understand this one must delve into the general theory of stochastic processes and understanding of fractal structures. Indeed the considerations presented in Chapter 2.5 do look suspiciously like fractal equations.[1]

Thus it appears that the theory (KVT) presented in this book albeit simplified and generalized is sufficiently close to explain and predict aspects of the SME world, it is not immediately scalable to encompass large organizations. However in his book *The Self Organizing Economy*, Paul Krugman (1996) also looks at bringing complex-systems analysis to economics, albeit in a more national economic perspective and several authors including Lee (2003) have started to address complexity theory and fuzzy logic applications in Human Resource Development. This implies that the time may be ripe, if the limitations described above can be satisfactorily addressed.

Convection in the DI net was mentioned above as a manifestation of gossip in small organizations. When progressing to large organization it can be assumed that the DI net will literally creak with turbulence. This is really not easy to model and the interested reader is referred to the classical works by Landau, Mandelbrot, Feigenbaum and others. An accessible starting point for Chaos Theory is Gleick (1987). Researchers taking KVT further may well find using concepts like Markov chains and neural networks useful.

---

[1] The general formula for fractal equations is $Z \rightarrow Z(\text{operator}) + \text{constant}$

15.3   Are charismatic leaders Strange Attractors?

An organization is a dynamic system and in the economic world – just as in the physical world – dynamic systems tend to be dissipative. That is, the motion would cease if it were not for some driving force. In physics dissipation may come from e.g. friction, whereas in economics it is transaction costs (the equivalent of friction, so to speak) that may be the major factor.

Thus a further interesting speculation concerns the Strange Attractors known from Chaos Theory. Strange Attractors are relatively stable areas around which chaos flows. Trajectories (in our case, nodes or knowledge) within a strange attractor appear to skip around randomly but points that do get close enough to the attractor remain close even when slightly disturbed or agitated by external factors. Are these points akin to the strange and charismatic leaders the business world sometimes throws up – Carnegie, Rockefeller, Branson and Gates? Have they – consciously or not – internalized (see Boisot, 1998 and section 1) some mysterious rule of knowledge management, like the scarecrow in the film Wizard of Oz who says 'I won't try to manage things because I can't think' ... do they manage (to manage) without conscious thought?

Those interested in the psychology of power, charisma and leadership may find the works of Alice Miller an interesting starting point.

15.4   Finally – non-IT measures in large organizations

We saw in Case 2 that simple HR measures can promote knowledge sharing by promoting inter-nodal contact in the KVT net. One obvious difference between SMEs and larger organizations is size, and with size comes accommodation: Larger organizations are more likely to inhabit purpose-made buildings. Architecture has been known for some time to promote knowledge-sharing and large organizations design buildings around getting people with unlike jobs and skills to mix. Fortunately the old habit of putting employees in cupboard-sized offices is also seriously on the wane and while not being a fan of huge open-plan spaces (all too often an excuse of crushing more people in – laconically called 'future expansion') it is obviously a good idea that especially new employees share an office with 2–3 existing employees to help their initial integration into Knowledge Valley, some organization encourage semi-formal 'mentors'.

Other simple measures can increase employee 'buy-in' to the organization. Such measures help align individual aims with corporate aims and strategy. One such measure is staff benefits in the non-salary area ('perks'). Serious perks like a free telephone or a free PC to aid telecommuting can significantly improve workforce loyalty. Many supermarket chains give their employees 20–25% discount on their food bill. Unfortunately marginal perks can provoke a rebound effect;

one large organization I am acquainted with hired an individual to specifically negotiate perks with surrounding businesses, the results being e.g. 5% discount at a local hairdresser and other similar offers. Employees rapidly tired of a multitude of marginal (bordering on the useless) 'bargains' and a popular groundswell of opinion formed stating that they would rather stop the perks and share out that persons salary instead, or at least use the salary to employ a useful co-worker who would share their work-load.

As noted in Chapter 9, there are also innovation-stopping measures in the non-IT area. Of these a bonus scheme weighted in favour of senior management could be an example. Certainly where senior management is on 'performance-related pay' the conditions exist for squeezing more out of employees, which is repaid in failing trust and eventually the information gatekeepers become divorced from the information and diversity innovation that they need.

However the take-home message is that IT is not a magic bullet that alone will promote knowledge-sharing, but rather only part of organization-wide measures to navigate to the profitable areas of Knowledge Valley. I wish to leave you with the thought that IT improves throughput (Case 1) in Boisot's I-space, thus promoting mutual inspiration ('diversity innovation', see Case 3) and hope you can see that KVT can usefully be applied to large organizations too.

literature cited

Allen, T. (1977). *Managing the flow of technology*. MIT Press.

Anderson, C. (2007). *The long tail*. Random House Business Books.

Angerhahn (1997). The ICDT model. Towards a taxonomy of Internet-related business strategies. INSEAD Working Paper series.

Argyris, M. and Schön, D. (1974) *Theory in practice. Increasing professional effectiveness*. Jossey-Bass.

Arrow, K. (1962). The economic implications of learning by doing. *Review of Economic Studies*, 29, 153–73.

Arundel, A., Van de Paal, G. & Soete, L. (1995). Innovation strategies of Europe's largest industrial firms. PACE Report, University of Limbourg.

Atherton, A. & Hannon, P. D. (2001). Innovation processes and the small business, a conceptual analysis. *International Journal of Business Performance Management*, 2, 276–92.

Baden-Fuller, C. & Pitt, M. (1996). *Strategic innovation*. Routledge, London.

Barnes, D., Dyerson, R., Harindranath, G., Dickson, K., Harris, L., Clear, F. et al. (2007). Abandoned heroes: ICT adoption and use in SMEs. KURIR-2007-W1. [available at http://kurir.kingston.ac.uk/AbandonedHeroes.pdf]

Barrow, C. (1998). *The essence of small business*. Prentice Hall.

Bass, F. M. (2004). Comments on a new product growth for model consumer durables. *Management Science*, 50, 1833–40.

Becker, S. W. & Whistler, T. L. (1967). The innovative organization, a selective view of current theory and research. *Journal of Business*, 40, 462–9.

Bell, D. (1973). *The coming of post-industrial society*. Basic Books.

Besanko, D., Dranove, D., Shanley, M. & Schaefer, S. (2007). *Economics of strategy*. John Wiley.

Bessant, J. (1999). Developing continuous improvement capability. *International Journal of Innovation Management*, 2, 409–29.

Bessant, J. & Tidd, J. (2007). *Innovation and entrepreneurship*. John Wiley.

Birch, D. L. (1987). *Job creation in America, how our smallest companies put the most people in work*. Free Press.

Birkinshaw, J. & Sheehan, T. (2002). *Managing the knowledge life cycle*. MIT Sloan Management Review, 75–83

Blackler, F. (1995). Knowledge, knowledge work and organizations. *Organization Studies*, 16, 1021–46.

Boisot, M. H. (1998). *Knowledge assets*. Oxford. Oxford University Press.

Bremmer, I. (2006). *The J Curve*. Simon and Schuster.

Burns, P. & Whitehouse, O. (1995). Financing in Europe 2. Milton Keynes. 3i Enterprise Centre.

Bygrave, W. D. & Timmons, J. A. (1992). Venture capital at the crossroads. Harvard Business School Press.

Cadle, J. & Yeats, D. (2008). *Project management and information systems* (5th edn). Prentice Hall.

Carneiro, A. (2000). How does knowledge management influence innovation and competitiveness? *Journal of Knowledge Management*, 4, 87–98.

Chandler, A. D. (1962). *Strategy and structure*. MIT Press.

Chaston, I. (2000). *Entrepreneurial marketing*. Macmillan.

Churchill, N. & Lewis, V. (1983). The five stages of small business growth. Harvard Small Business Review, 61, May/June, 30–50.

Cole-Gomolski, B. (1997). Users loath to share their knowledge. *Computerworld*, 31, 46.

Covin, J. G. & Slevin, D. P. (1998). Strategic behaviour of small firms in hostile and benign environments. *Strategic management journal*, 10, 75–87.

Daft, R. L. & Becker, S. W. (1978). *Innovation in organizations*. Elsevier.

Davenport, T. H. & Prusak, L. (1998). *Working knowledge*. (2nd revised edn 2000). Harvard Business School Press.

Davies, J. C. (1962). Towards a theory of revolution. *American Sociological Review*, 27, 5–18.

Davis, F. D. (1989). Perceived usefulness, perceived ease of use and user acceptance of information technology. *MIS Quarterly*, 13/3, 319–40.

Davis, J. P., Bingham, C. B. & Eisenhardt, K. M. (2007). Developing theory through simulation models. *Academy of Management Review*, 32, 480–99.

DeBono, E. (1996). *Serious creativity*. Harper Collins.

Deem, R., Hillyard, S. & Reed, M. (2007). *Knowledge, higher education, and the new managerialism*. Oxford University Press.

DeLong, D. W. (2004). *Lost knowledge*. Oxford University Press.

Diegel, O. (2005). Breaking down innovation: New tools for project managing innovative projects. *The Innovation Journal: The Public Sector Innovation Journal*, 10, 33.

Downs, G. R. Jr & Mohr, L. B. (1976). Toward a theory of innovation. *Administration and Society*, 10, 379–408.

Dreyfus, H. L. (2001). *On the Internet*. Routledge.

Dreyfus, H. L. & Dreyfus, S. E. (1986). *Mind over machine*. Free Press.

Drucker, P. F. (1985). *Innovation and entrepreneurship*. Butterworth-Heinemann.

Drucker, P. F. (1993). *Post-capitalist society*. Butterworth-Heinemann.

Dubash, M. (2005). Moore's Law is dead, says Gordon Moore. Techworld. http://www.techworld.com/opsys/news/index.cfm?NewsID=3477. Retrieved on 02.01.2009.

Dunn, S. (2004). *Philosophical foundations of education: connecting philosophy to theory and practice*. Prentice Hall.

Etllie, J. (2000). *Managing technological innovation*. John Wiley.

EU. COMMISSION OF THE EUROPEAN COMMUNITIES (2005). Report on the implementation of the European Charter for Small Enterprises. http://europa.eu.int/comm/enterprise/enterprise_policy/charter/charter_en.pdf

Farrell , M. A. (2000). Developing a market-oriented learning organisation. *Australian Journal of Management*, 25, 201–23 (available on www.agsm.unsw.edu.au/eajm/0009/farrell.html).

Galbraith, J. K. (1967). *The new industrial state*. Boston. Houghton Miffin.

Gardner, H. (1983). *Frames of mind*. Basic Books.

Garnsey, E. (1996). *A new theory of the growth of the firm*. 4. Stockholm, ICSB 41st World Conference.

Gelepithis, P. A. M. (2005). Knowledge, IT and the firm. In M. Khosrow-Pour (ed.) Encyclopedia of Information Science and Technology, 1783–7. Idea Group Reference.

Gleick, J. A. (1987). *Chaos*. Sphere Books.

Gourlay, S. (2006). Conceptualizing knowledge creation, a critique of Nonakas theory. *Journal of Management Studies*, 43, 1415–36.

Gopalakrishnan, S. & Bierly, P. (2001). Analysing innovation adoption using a knowledge-based approach. *Journal Of Engineering And Technology Management*, 18, 107–30.

Granovetter, M. (1973). The strength of weak ties. *American Journal of Sociology*, 78, 1360–80.

Granovetter, M. (1983). The strength of the weak tie revisited. *Sociological Theory*, 1, 201–33.

Granovetter, M. (2004). The impact of social structure on economic outcomes. *Journal of Economic Perspectives*, 19, 33–50.

Grant, R. (1996). Prospering in dynamically competitive environments. *Organization Science*, 7, 375–87.

Greenberg, J. & Baron, R. (2000). *Behaviour in organizations* (7th edn). Prentice-Hall.

Greiner, L. (1972). Evolution and revolution as organisations grow. *Harvard Business Review*, 50, July/August, 37–46.

Haldane, J. B. S. (1985). *On being the right size*. Oxford University Press (originally published 1928).

Hansen, M. T., Nohria, N. & Tierney, T. (1999). What is your strategy for managing knowledge? *Harvard Business Review*, March–April. 106–16.

Heines, M. H. (2007). *Patents for Business*. Praeger Publishers.

Henderson, R. M., Clark, K. B. (1990). Architectural innovation: The reconfiguration of existing product technologies and the failure of established firms. *Administrative Science Quarterly*, 35, 9–30.

Holmes, S. & Zimmer, I. (1994). The nature of the small firm: understanding the motivations of growth and non-growth oriented owners. *Australian Journal of Management*, 19, 97–120.

Horton, W. (2000). *Designing web based training*. J. Wiley.

Huysman, M. & de Wit, D. (2004). Practices of managing knowledge sharing: Towards a second wave of knowledge management. *Knowledge & Process Management*, 11, 81–92.

Iansiti, M. (1993). Real world R&D; jumping the product generation gap. *Harvard Business Review*, 71, 138–47.

Ingham, G. (1979). *Size of industrial organization and worker behaviour*. Cambridge University Press.

Jarvis, P. (2003). *The theory and practice of learning* (2nd edn). Routledge Falmer.

Kanter, R. M. (1983). The change masters; innovation and productivity in the American corporation. Simon & Schuster.

Katz, R. (2004). The motivation of professionals. In, Katz, R. (ed.), *The human side of managing technological innovation*. Oxford University Press. pp. 3–20.

Kelly, K. (1998). *New rules for the new economy*. New York. Penguin.

Kelly, W. W. (1991). Directions in the anthropology of contemporary Japan. *Annual Review of Anthropology*, 20, 395–431.

Kirby, D. A. (2003). *Entrepreneurship*. McGraw-Hill.

Kirton, M. J. (2003). *Adaption-Innovation in the context of diversity and change*. Routledge.

Knight, K. (1967). A descriptive model of the intra-firm innovation process. *Journal of Business*, 40, 478–96.

Kogut, B. & Zander, U. (1992). Knowledge of the firm; combination, capabilities and the replication of technology. *Organization Science*, 3, 383–97.

Kondratieff, N. D. (1935). The long waves in economic life. *Review of Economics and Statistics*, 17, 105–15 (originally published in 1926 in Archiv für Sozialwissenschaft und Socialpolitik).

Kotler, P. & Armstrong, G. (1989). *Principles of marketing* (4th edn). Prentice-Hall.

Kotler, P. & Trias de Bes, F. (2003). *Lateral marketing*. John Wiley.

Krugman, P. (1996). *The self-organizing economy*. Wiley-Blackwell.

Lagerström, K. L. & Andersson, M. (2003). Creating and sharing knowledge within a transnational team, the development of a global business system. *Journal of World Business*, 38, 84–95.

Leadbeater, C. (2009). *We-Think: mass innovation not mass production*. Profile Books.

Lee, A. S. (2001). Editor's Comments. *MIS Quarterly*, 25, iii–vii.

Lee, M. (2003). *HRD in a complex world*. Routledge.

Leong, A. (1998). The ICDT Model: A framework for e-business. www.mediacircus.net/icdt.html

Levine, R & Locke, C. (2009). *The Cluetrain Manifesto*. Basic Books.

Liebowitz, J. (2002). Knowledge mapping; an essential part of knowledge management. In, White, D. (ed.) *Knowledge mapping and management*. IRM Press. pp. 23–9.

Lillrank, P. & Holopainen, S. (1998). Reengineering for business option value. *Journal of Organizational Change Management*, 11, 246–59.

Magretta, J. (1998). Governing the family owned enterprise, an interview with Finlands Krister Ahlstrom. *Harvard Business Review*, Jan–Feb. 113–23.

Mahajan, V., Muller, E. & Bass, F. M. (1990). New product diffusion models in marketing, a review and directions for research. *Journal of Marketing*, 54, 1–26.

Marr, B. & Spender, J-C. (2004). Measuring knowledge assets – implications of the knowledge economy for performance measurement. *Measuring Business Excellence*, 8, 18–27.

Mascitelli, R. (2000). From experience: Harnessing tacit knowledge to achieve break-through innovation. *Journal of Product Innovation Management*, 17, 179–93.

Mazzarol, T. (2003). A model of small business HR growth management. *International Journal of Entrepreneurial Behaviour & Research*, 9, 27–49.

McAdam, R. & Reid, R. (2001). SME and large organization perceptions of knowledge management. *Journal of Knowledge Management*, 3, 231–41.

McAfee, A. P. (2006). Enterprise 2.0: The dawn of emergent collaboration. *MIT Sloan Management Review*, 47, 21–8.

McDonald, M & Christopher, M. (2003). *Marketing, a complete guide*. Palgrave.

McLean, J. E. & Mellor, R. B. (2006). The identification of XML-related skills gaps in the aerospace & defence industry in the West Focus region. KURIR-2006-W1 [available at http://kurir.kingston.ac.uk/Report_XML_skill_shortage.pdf]

McMahon, R. G. P. (1998). Stage models of SME growth reconsidered. Flinders Business School, School of Commerce Research Paper Series. Available at http://commerce.flinders.edu.au/researchpapers/98–5.htm.

Mellor, R. B. (2003a). *Innovation management*. Globe.

Mellor, R. B. (2003b). *The web managers handbook*. Globe.

Mellor, R. B. (2005a). *Sources and spread of innovation in small e-commerce companies*. Globe.

Mellor, R. B. (2005b). Achieving Enterprise: Teaching entrepreneurship and innovation in business and academia. FGF Entrepreneurship Research Monographs, 49, Eul Verlag.

Mellor, N. & Mellor, R. B. (2004). *Applied e-learning*. Globe.

Mellor, R. B. (2008). *Entrepreneurship for everyone*. Sage.

Mintzberg, H. (1979). *Structures in fives, designing effective organizations*. Prentice-Hall.

Mintzberg, H. (1988). The change cube. In, Mintzberg, H., Ahlstrand, B. & Lempel, J. (eds) *Strategy safari*. Free Press.

Montgomery, J. D. (1992). Job search and network composition: Implications of the strength of weak ties hypothesis. *American Sociological Review*, 57, 586–96.

Moore, G. (1995). *Inside the tornado*. Harper Business.

Newell, S., Robertson, M., Scarborough, H., & Swan, J. (2009). *Managing knowledge work and innovation*. Palgrave.

Nissen, M. (2008) Streams of shared knowledge: Computational expansion of knowledge-flow theory. *Knowledge Management Research & Practice*, 6, 124–40.

Nonaka, I. & Takeuchi, H. (1995). *The knowledge-creating company*. Oxford University Press.

Ormerod, P. (2005). *Why most things fail*. Faber and Faber.

Ozmon, H. A. & Craver, S. M. (2003). *Philosophical foundations of education*. Prentice Hall.

Palmer, A. (2004). *Introduction to marketing theory and practice* (2nd edn). Oxford, Oxford University Press.

Parkhurst, H. B. (1999). Confusion, lack of consensus and the definition of creativity as a construct. *Journal of Creative Behaviour*, 33, 1–21.

Penrose, E. (1995). *The theory and growth of the firm*. Oxford University Press.

Pierce, J. L. & Delbecq, A. L. (1977). Organizational structure, individual attitudes and innovation. *Academy of Management Journal*, 2, 27–37.

Poltorak, A. I. & Lerner, P. J. (2004). Essentials of licensing intellectual property. John Wiley.

Porter, M. E. (1980). *Competitive strategy*. The Free Press

Porter, M. E. (1990). *The competitive advantage of nations*. Palgrave.

Prescott, M. B. & Van Slyke, C. (1996). The Internet as innovation. http://hsb.baylor.edu/ramsower/ais.ac.96/papers/prescott.htm

Quinn, J. B. & Hilmer, F. G. (1995). Strategic outsourcing. *McKinsey Quarterly*, 1, 48–70.

Ram, M. (1994). *Managing to survive, working lives in small firms*. Blackwell.

Rapoport, A. (1957). Contributions to the theory of random and biased nets. *Bulletin of Mathematical Biophysics*, 19, 257–77.

Raymond, E. (2001). *The cathedral and the bazaar*. O'Reilly.

Rayport, J. F. & Sviokla, J. J. (1995). Exploiting the virtual value chain. *Harvard Business Review*, 73, 75–85.

Rogers, E. M. (1983). *Diffusion of innovations*. The Free Press.

Rothwell, R. (1992). Successful industrial innovation: Critical success factors for the 1990s. *R&D Management*, 22, 221–39.

Salomon, G. (1979). Interaction of media, cognition and learning. Jossey-Bass. (Published again by Lawrence Erlbaum, 1994).

Safko, L. & Brake, D. (2009). *The social media Bible: tactics, tools, and strategies for business success*. John Wiley.

Schumpeter, J. A. (1912). *Theorie der wirtschaftlichen Entwicklung*. Leipzig. (Duncker & Humblot, 5th edn, 1952).

Schumpeter, J. A. (1939). *Business cycles: A theoretical, historical, and statistical analysis of the capitalist process*. McGraw Hill.

Segaran, T. (2007). *Programming collective intelligence: Building Smart Web 2.0 Applications*. O'Reilly.

Schumpeter, J. A. (1942). *Capitalism, socialism and democracy*. Harper.

Shannon, C. E. (1948). A mathematical theory of communication. *Bell System Technical Journal*, 27, 379–423.

Shannon, C. E. & Weaver, W. (1963). *The mathematical theory of communication*. University of Illinois Press.

Shepard. H. A. (1967). Innovation-resisting and innovation-producing organizations. *Journal of Business*, 40, 470–77.

Shoham, Y. & Leyton-Brown, K. (2008). *Multiagent systems: Algorithmic, game-theoretic, and logical foundations*. Cambridge University Press.

Slevin, D. P. & Covin, J. G. (1990). Juggling entrepreneurial style and organizational structure, how to get your act together. *Sloan Management Review*, winter, 43–53.

Sparrow, J. (2001). Knowledge management in small firms. *Knowledge and Process Management*, 8, 3–16.

Spender, J-C. (1998). Pluralist epistemology and the knowledge-based theory of the firm. *Organization*, 5, 233–56.

Stacey, R. D. (1996). *Complexity and creativity in organizations*. Berrett-Koehler Publishers.

Starbuck, W. (1992). Learning by knowledge-intensive firms. *Journal of Management Studies*, 29, 713–40.

Stokes, D. (2002). *Small business management* (4th edn). Thomson.

Storey, D. J. (1994). *Understanding small firms*. Routledge.

Surowiecki, J. (2005). *The wisdom of crowds*. Anchor Books (Reprint edition).

Tampoe, M. (1993). *Motivating knowledge workers*. Long Range Planning, 26, 49–55.

Tapscott, D. & Williams, A. (2008). *Wikinomics*. Atlantic Books.

Teece, D. J. (2000). *Managing intellectual capital*. Oxford University Press.

Thompson. V. A. (1965). *Bureaucracy and innovation*. Administrative Science Quarterly, 5, 1–20.

Thompson, M. P. A. & Walsham, G. (2004). Placing knowledge management in context. *Journal of Management Studies*, 4, 725–47.

Tidd, J., Bessand, J. & Pavitt, K. (2001). *Managing innovation*. Wiley.

Turban, E. & Volonino, L. (2010). *Information technology for management*. Wiley.

Utterback, J. M. (1994). *Mastering the dynamics of innovation*. Harvard Business School Press.

Williams, G. P. (1997). *Chaos theory tamed*. Washington, DC: National Academies Press.

Williamson, O. E. (1995). *The economic institutions of capitalism*. The Free Press.

Williamson, O. E. & Masten, S. E. (1999). The economics of transaction costs. Edward Elgar Publishing.

Wilson, T. D. (2002). The nonsense of 'knowledge management'. Information Research, 8, paper no. 144 [Available at http://InformationR.net/ir/8–1/paper144.html]

Valery, N. (1999). Innovation in industry. *Economist*, 5, 28.

Van Grundy. A. (1987). Organisational creativity and innovation. In, S. G. Isaksen (ed.), *Frontiers of creativity research*. Brearly.

Von Hippel, E. (1994). Sticky information and problem solving. *Management Science*, 40, 429–439

Vyakarnham, S. & Leppard, J. (1999). *A marketing action plan for growing companies*. Kogan Page.

Yee, R. (2008). *Pro Web 2.0 Mashups: Remixing Data and Web Services*, Apress.

Zaltman, G., Duncan, R. & Holbeck, L. (1973). *Innovation in organizations*. John Wiley.

appendix 1: useful web links

This list is neither exhaustive nor a recommendation, and should be used purely for guidance and inspiration.

Theme	Domain name
Association for Information Systems	isworld.org
CRM	Ecrmguide.com and crm-forum.com
Decision support	tradeportal.com
Open Applications Group (OAGI)	openapplications.org
Joint Information Systems Committee	jisc.ac.uk
Project management	citadon.com
Resources for IT managers	cio.com and information-age.com
Software	Tucows.com, 2020software.com and findaccountingsoftware.com
Not-for-profit DSDM Consortium	dsdm.org
Transaction Processing Performance Council	tpc.org
Microsoft Technet	technet.microsoft.com
Google Technology User Groups	gtugs.org

appendix 2: glossary

API
Application Programming Interface is the way in which one piece of software (a programme) asks another programme to perform a service.

ATM
An Automated Teller Machine (ATM) sometimes called Automatic Banking Machine (ABM), or 'a cash machine' in common parlance, is a networked computerized device that provides clients of a financial institution with access to financial transactions in a public space (i.e. not Internet banking) without the need for a cashier, human clerk or bank teller to be present.

BPR
Business Process Reengineering (BPR) is the analysis and redesign of workflow within and between enterprises, with outcomes (as opposed to tasks) as the central theme. Over-zealous application and workforce resistance modified this to remodelling as well as enhance expectations for a successor, which many thought of as being enterprise resource planning (ERP).

CMS
Content Management System is a server-based software system to manage the content of a website. A CMS allows the content manager or author to manage the creation, modification and removal of content from a website without needing the expertise of a Webmaster.

CRM
An information system – often integrated into an intranet – used to plan, schedule and control the presales and post-sales activities of an organization e.g. dealing with prospects and customers, and organizing sales force activities, marketing, technical support and field service.

DI number
Diversity Innovation number, the number of ties between nodes (people) in a Knowledge Valley net.

DoI Theory
Diffusion of Innovations Theory is, in the words of Everett Rogers, 'the process by which an innovation is communicated through certain channels over time among the members of a social system'.

DSDM
Dynamic Systems Development Method is an iterative and incremental approach to software development that emphasizes continuous user involvement in a context of changing

requirements along the development process. DSDM is closely associated with Agile Development.

ECDL
European Computer Drivers Licence is a European qualification demonstrating basic competence in common computer skills.

Entrepreneurship
Entrepreneurship is defined as an academic discipline in management and economics. In the framework of economics, entrepreneurship is an important exception to classical input–output economics.

ERP
Enterprise Resource Planning is a business management system integrating many different aspects of the business, like planning, manufacturing, sales, inventory control, order tracking, customer service, finance, human resources and marketing.

GDP
Gross Domestic Product is the annual value of a country's overall production of goods and services (source: dictionary.com).

GIS
Geographical Information Systems capture, manage, analyse and display all forms of geographically referenced information (source: GIS.com).

GPS
Global Positioning Systems is a radio-navigation system provided by orbital satellites that broadcast their position, the receivers' position being then calculated by passive devices, e.g. a sat-nav or similar, using triangulation between the satellites.

HR(M)
Human Resources (Management) is an organizational function that deals with issues related to people such as compensation, hiring, performance management, organization development, safety, wellness, benefits, employee motivation, communication, administration and training (source: about.com).

ICDT Theory
virtual Information space, virtual Communication space, virtual Distribution space and virtual Transaction space as pertaining to e-commerce.

Innovation
Innovation is a new way of doing something and may refer to incremental or radical and revolutionary changes in thinking, products, processes or organizations. The goal of innovation is positive change; to make someone or something better. Innovation leading to increased productivity is the fundamental source of increasing wealth in an economy or organization (source: Wikipedia).

IP(R)
Intellectual Property (Rights) refers to creations of the mind: inventions, literary and artistic works, and symbols, names, images and designs used in commerce (source: wipo.int).

I-Space
Information Space, is a 3D modelling of the political economy of knowledge as proposed in 1998 by Prof Max Boisot.

ITIL
Information Technology Infrastructure Library is guidance on the provision of quality and support for IT services, and on the accommodation and environmental facilities needed to support IT. It is based on British Standards Institution's Standard for IT Service Management (BS15000) and later ISO 20,000.

Knowledge Management
Knowledge Management refers to the strategies and practices used in an organization to identify, create, represent, distribute and enable adoption of insights and experiences. Such insights and experiences comprise knowledge, either embodied in individuals or embedded in organizational processes or practice.

KVT
Knowledge Valley Theory derives its name from the 'valley', a 3D fold, formed after plotting the theoretical DI number in an organization against number of employees and against profitability (or annual turnover).

Mashup
Mashups are web pages or applications that use/combines data or functionality from two (or indeed many more) external sources to create a new service.

NGO
A Non-Governmental Organization is a legally constituted organization created by natural or legal persons without any government participation. In practice the term NGO often refers to a pressure or consultative organization, one flavour of which is QUANGO, a quasi-autonomous non-governmental organization, or an NGO to which a government has devolved power.

PERT
Program Evaluation Review Technique, a methodology to manage large and complex projects: Similar to the Critical Path Method (CPM).

PRINCE 2
(PRojects IN Controlled Environments) is a process-based method for effective project management. PRINCE2 is a Trade Mark of the Office of Government Commerce (source: prince2.com).

RoI
Return on Investment is a measure of how effectively an organization utilizes its investment to generate profit.

RSS
Really Simple Syndication is an XML-based vocabulary for distributing Web content in opt-in feeds, thereby allowing a user to have new content delivered to a computer or mobile device as soon as it is published instead of visiting multiple Web pages to check for new content.

SaaS
Software as a service is the concept of software provided as needed. This could be applications for e.g. office work or e.g. cloud-based databases. This concept is popular as it leaves a zero IT-footprint in the organization and thus is relatively inexpensive.

SBS
Social Business Systems are internal organizational instances of Social Network Systems (SNS).

SECI cycle
Socialization (tacit to tacit), Externalization (from tacit to explicit), Combination (explicit to explicit) and Internalization (explicit to tacit). A knowledge cycle first propounded in 1995 by Nonaka and Takeuchi.

SLC
Social Learning Cycle is the preferred path around the I-Space taken by social and generational knowledge and insights. The six-stage model was proposed in 1998 by Boisot.

SME
Small and Medium sized Enterprise. An organization employing maximum 249 employees.

SMS
Short Messaging Service is a text-based communication service component of the mobile telephone/communication system.

SNS
Social Network Systems are world-wide Internet-mediated social circles or networks. SNS web sites are epitomized by e.g. Friendster.

SoA
Service-oriented Architecture is a flexible set of design principles (i.e. defining the interface in terms of protocols and functionality) used during systems development and integration.

SOAP
Simple Object Access Protocol is a protocol specification for exchanging structured information and providing a basic messaging framework upon which web services can be built.

SQL
Standard Query Language is an international standard for inserting and retrieving data from databases.

SSADM
Structured Systems Analysis and Design Method was developed on behalf of the British government in the 1980s and was declared as the standard to be applied to development projects of the British government. SSADM is a top-down approach applied to IT development projects where the methodology does not need to address areas beyond analysis and design (i.e. no deployment or implementation).

SW Theory
The theory that the development of the Internet occurs in cycles, alternating between time saving (S) and time wasting (W) activities.

TCP/IP
Transmission Control Protocol (TCP) and the Internet Protocol (IP) are the communication protocol for the Internet and define the rule computers must follow to communicate with each other over the Internet.

TQM
Total Quality Management is a management concept aiming to reduce errors during the manufacturing or service process by including workforce feedback and participation (see also 'Quality Circle' and Kaizen) in order to increase customer satisfaction, to streamline supply chain management and so on.

UDDI
Universal Description, Discovery and Integration is an XML-based Service Registry for organizations to list themselves on the Internet. UDDI is an open industry initiative, sponsored by the Organization for the Advancement of Structured Information Standards (OASIS), enabling businesses to publish service listings and discover each other and define how the services or software applications interact over the Internet (source: uddi.xml.org).

UML
The Unified Modelling Language (presently in version 2) is used to specify, visualize, modify, construct and document the time-dependant architecture of a project, including the relationships between the various entities, as well as the business process flow.

VAT
Value Added Tax is a form of indirect sales tax or Government levy on the amount a firm adds to the price of a goods or services as value is added, although in principal it should act mainly on the end-user in domestic consumption.

VoIP
Voice-over Internet Protocols is the protocol used for computers to translate analogue speech into digital format for sending as packets over a data network like the Internet and to then convert it back at the other end. Thus VoIP allows one to make telephone calls through a computer.

Web 2.0
Web2 is a diffuse term generally meaning web applications that facilitate interactive information sharing, interoperability, user-centred design and collaboration on the World Wide Web.

Web Ontology Language (OWL)
Used where information contained in documents needs to be processed by computer applications (as opposed to humans). OWL stipulates vocabularies and the relationships between specified terms (i.e. ontology). The name of an owl character in Winnie the Pooh books is (mis)spelt WOL, hence the not-immediately-obvious abbreviation.

WSDL
Web Services Description Language is an XML-based language that provides a model for describing Web services. The meaning of the acronym has changed from version 1.1 where the D stood for Definition (source: Wikipedia).

XML
eXtensible Markup Language is an open-standard set of rules for encoding documents electronically, often with HTML-like tags. XML's design goals emphasize simplicity, generality and usability over the Internet. Although XML's design focuses on documents, it is widely used for the representation of arbitrary data structures, where the tag structure mirrors the database structure. To date hundreds of XML-based languages have been developed, of which the most relevant here may be XBRL (eXtensible Business Reporting Language).

appendix 3: exercises

Exercise 1: Making a mashup

A suggestion for coursework or project could be to make a mashup for a real or fictitious business. With these tools that you will be able to build your own systems based upon many of Google's familiar services and data such as Maps, Search and Analytics, or begin exploring Cloud Computing or Mobile.

This coursework suggestion is the modification of the results of a unique collaboration between Google UK and Kingston University (the original is at http://docs.google.com/ View?id=dgztgs7b_1737ng66dj) aimed at final year Information Systems students. This example should contain enough information and pointers to help you evaluate a range of technologies and decide whether they fit into your project plans. We've tried to provide plenty of ideas for projects and tips for getting the best out of your project. Don't be overwhelmed by all the links and tools available, the key will be to browse some of the tools and suggestions and then to imagine how these could contribute to your projects ... take it to the next level!

What is Google's developer strategy?

- Google wants the web to be the programming platform of the future: It's open and is built on standards that are becoming more ubiquitous.
- Google's mission is to be able to provide the tools for a small group of developers to build the next Gmail (or mobile maps application) as opposed to a large (50+) team.
- Google invests millions of dollars per annum in this area, opening up infrastructure developed to host its own apps (Search, Gmail & App Engine), licensing data for own products then opening it all up to developers (Maps API etc.).
- Why? Because if the web becomes better, more people will spend more time on it (and more people will come online). This in turn will lead to more searches and this means more revenue.

What Google developer products are available today?

Here are just some of the many APIs and tools available to you to use:

1. **Tools to build and host applications or data:**
   - App Engine: http://code.google.com/appengine/docs/whatisgoogleappengine.html
   - Google Web Toolkit http://code.google.com/webtoolkit/overview.html
   - Google Base http://code.google.com/apis/base/
   - App engine/web tool kit/web development intro – http://www.youtube.com/watch?v=koKaH_r_DaY&feature=channel
   - extending Google apps – http://dl.google.com/gdd/2009/intl/cs/GDD2009_Extending_Google_Apps.pdf

2. **Tools to enrich sites:**
    A. AJAX APIs (Maps, search etc.) http://code.google.com/apis/ajax
    B. Language Tools http://code.google.com/apis/ajaxlanguage and
    C. http://dl.google.com/gdd/2009/intl/cs/GDD2009_EMEA-DevelopandDeployYou rNextAJAXApplicationintheCloud.pdf
    D. and http://dl.google.com/gdd/2009/intl/cs/GDD2009-GWT_App-Architecture-Best-Practices.pdf
    E. Http://dl.google.com/gdd/2009/intl/cs/GDD2009_GoogleWaveClientGWT.pdf 234458.
    G. Chrome/extensions – http://www.youtube.com/watch?v=-N_EpuoZmaw& feature = channel and http://dl.google.com/gdd/2009/intl/cs/GDD2009-Chrome-Extensions.pdf
    H. chrome developer tools – http://dl.google.com/gdd/2009/intl/cs/GDD2009_Chrome_DevTools.pdf

3. **Tools to mine data or provide business intelligence**
    - Analytics API http://code.google.com/apis/analytics/
    - Adwords API http://code.google.com/apis/adwords/docs/developer/index.html
    - GViz http://code.google.com/apis/visualization/
    - traffic generation – http://dl.google.com/gdd/2009/intl/cs/GDD2009-Driving-Users.pdf and http://www.youtube.com/watch?v=HfhhLnhmHqc&feature=channel
    - metrics and website optimiser and other apis (maps, video, ajax search, ajax feeds, language) – http://dl.google.com/gdd/2009/intl/cs/GDD2009-Engage-Users.pdf

4. **Tools to bridge the gap with mobile**
    - Android http://developer.android.com/index.html
    - android – http://dl.google.com/gdd/2009/intl/cs/GDD2009-Android-for-Beginners. pdf and http://www.youtube.com/watch?v=DSMriibR99E&feature=channel
    - Mobile web – http://dl.google.com/gdd/2009/intl/cs/GDD2009-Building-High-Performance-Mobile-Web-Applications.pdf

5. **3D and Geo**
    - wave APIs – http://dl.google.com/gdd/2009/intl/cs/GDD2009-Google-Wave-API. pdf
    - geo – http://dl.google.com/gdd/2009/intl/cs/GDD2009-Geo.pdf and http://www. youtube.com/watch?v=-eDGb1mj96I and http://www.youtube.com/ watch?v=4oGNfUkxg6g
    - http://www.youtube.com/watch?v=bqYkyLslniQ

6. **Tools to make the web more social**
    - Friend Connect http://code.google.com/apis/friendconnect/
    - OpenSocial http://code.google.com/apis/opensocial/
    - The open and social web – http://dl.google.com/gdd/2009/intl/cs/GDD2009-OpenSocialWeb.pdf
    - http://dl.google.com/gdd/2009/intl/cs/GDD2009_EMEA-DevelopandDeployYour NextAJAXApplicationintheCloud.pdf
    - http://dl.google.com/gdd/2009/intl/cs/GDD2009-GWT_App-Architecture-Best-Practices.pdf
    - http://dl.google.com/gdd/2009/intl/cs/GDD2009_GoogleWaveClientGWT.pdf

7. **Working to move the web forward**
   - HTML 5 http://googlecode.blogspot.com/2009/09/video-introduction-to-html-5.html
   - cloud computing/virtualisation backgrounder – http://dl.google.com/gdd/2009/intl/cs/GDD2009-Cloud-Computing-and-Virtualization.pdf

Ten sample uses of the APIs

1. Translate from Spanish into English http://code.google.com/apis/ajax/playground/?exp=language#translate
2. Show a map based on latitude and longitude http://code.google.com/apis/ajax/playground/?exp=language#map_simple
3. Make simple views in Android http://developer.android.com/guide/tutorials/views/index.html
4. Data visualization using a Map and the Visualization API http://code.google.com/apis/visualization/documentation/gallery/intensitymap.html
5. Friend Connect integration examples http://www.ossamples.com/api/
6. Experiment with layouts using the Ajax Search API http://code.google.com/apis/ajax/playground/#tabbed_display_mode
7. Integrate video into custom search results http://code.google.com/apis/ajax/playground/#youtube_channels
8. Recreate a mail application in GWT http://gwt.google.com/samples/Mail/Mail.html
9. An invention generator web app in HTML 5 http://eurekaapp.com/generate
10. MailChimp Google Analytics integration http://www.mailchimp.com/features/power_features/analytics360

Twenty ideas for projects

Remember that it is up to you to select your own project, discuss it with potential supervisors and advisors and involve a client if you want to. You are also responsible for checking that the ideas are suitable for the degree you are following, so read your project requirements carefully.

Below are a set of ideas that came from brainstorming meetings at Google and at Kingston University. Many of them are in the e-commerce area but they may spark off other ideas that you would prefer to do. They are not supposed to be titles but starting points for you to make your own.

1. Developing a Prototype for an Intelligent Product Recommendation Engine (Keywords: Pattern Detection, Data Mining/Clustering, Collective Intelligence, Personalized Marketing).
2. Visualization of Key Performance Indicators using Analytics – project driven from what is available inside analytics.
3. Visualization of e-commerce data using the Chart API.
4. Mashing up keyword demand and analytics data to suggest adwords campaigns.
5. Create a strategy dashboard for a company, based on analytics and other data – a project driven from KPIs identified by client.
6. Using GoogleBase to store data from an e-commerce client to allow additional (search) functionality on e-commerce site or intranet.
7. Enhancing product search results for an e-commerce client.
8. Intelligent store finders (using Geo APIs).

9. Optimising Adsense for a publisher like Palgrave through feedback and experimentation with keywords.
10. Adwords optimization experiments – and tie this in to intelligent bid strategies.
11. Application of translation tools to enable customer service/shopping.
12. Better reporting on search/checkout funnels through the Analytics API.
13. Product buzz detector – find out which of your products are increasing in popularity on the web.
14. Mobile visualization of data.
15. Creating brand experiences for a client in HTML 5 (instead of Flash).
16. Adding social tools to a client website to build audience.
17. Visualizing geospatial data such as journeys to work on Google Maps.
18. Mobile customer service tools.
19. Designing widgets to help customer decisions.
20. Deploying distributed applications in the cloud ... especially gCloud.

How to choose an interesting project from the above list.

- Watch the video/read the material about why APIs are interesting.
- Read through the list of projects – is there a connection with your placement company or a company you know? Does one just sound exciting? Can you find a client yourself who would be interested in one of the suggested ideas?
- Write down a list of questions that arise from one or more of the suggested project topics to help you narrow down your choice.
- Research the answers to the questions using the web before discussing with your supervisor/advisor – what would you do with the idea?
- Try and combine the ideas suggested in the titles with your own ideas to make this your own project.
- Try and work out three versions of what you would need to deliver: a small prototype, a working proof of concept and a full scale demonstration/system.
- Write down the different deliverables for each of these three versions – this will help you plan the route through your project. Remember the time available to your project.
- While you are research the suggested topics you will probably stumble over other ideas that may be even better. Research these and then discuss with your supervisor.
- A great project has a straightforward first step and many different endings, often depending on what your initial experiments reveal.

Some advice from inside Google.

A. If you are working with a company make sure that the company can be flexible (code, business, timescales, expenses).
B. Try and fix things that are practical – fix the basics first
C. Make sure that your solution is scalable and changable – don't make your interface too rigid.
D. Beware of Beta APIs because they could be changed at any time; try to use an AGILE (see DSDM) approach.
E. Invent a 'hello world' for the API before embarking on a bigger project.
F. Augment your programming skills with specialist skills in testing, optimization or analytics.

G. Make things very easy for clients to implement – don't create huge pieces of code. Lightweight is better!
H. Use A/B testing to demonstrate the value of what you are doing.
 I. Collaborate with others working on similar projects – make sure your bit is clear.
 J. Consider using the cloud-based hosting for storing and scaling your application.

Working with the APIs

- Using APIs is not copying or cheating. Every university wants to ensure that work you claim to be yours really is and will use anti-plagiarism tools (e.g. turnitin) to check. Building your own software using the APIs is not plagiarism as long as the code you create is yours and you demonstrate in your documentation how you have used third party services such as those provided by Google. Check with your supervisor or advisor that you are documenting this in the right way.
- Read the terms and conditions. Make sure that you read the terms and conditions for each API you use. A few of them cost money (but most are free). A few are highly experimental and may change while you are doing your project.
- Work with your supervisor. These technologies are often very new and you cannot expect your supervisors to have used them themselves. This may put some students off using the APIs but that would be a mistake. See your supervisor as someone with whom you can explore the technology together.
- Can I get away with using mashups/web services rather than building something from scratch? Your project is not necessarily easier just because you are using tools from Google. You are just starting further down the road and this should allow you to achieve more within the timeframe for your project.

What to do when things don't work as you expected.

- Don't expect things to work without effort and don't give up too quickly.
- Copy any error messages into Google and see whether other people have had the same problem.
- Find the forums and groups that work with the APIs you are using; most of the links above contain a link to the appropriate group.
- Simplify the problem; stripping it back until it works. Go right back to 'hello world' if necessary.
- Explain what you are doing to a friend; this often helps expose an error in your logic.
- Use the tools built into your development environment or IDE to step through your code.
- Share your successes in solving problems through your blog and by participating in the appropriate groups.
- Document how you solved these problems as part of your final report

Tips for getting the best from your project.

- Set up a project blog to tell people about your project – this will help you document what you are doing and to blog recommendations.
- Link to other current project blogs and work your network for ideas. Use tools such as Twitter and LinkedIn to tell the world what you are doing.
- Use Google Docs and Spreadsheets to share ideas with your supervisor.

Feedback

All feedback is welcome. Pease contact Dr. Robert Mellor, Kingston University (you're going to have to Google that) and he will pass ideas onto the rest of the team.

PLEASE NOTE: We cannot however answer ANY individual technical questions. For these refer to the help section in the appropriate part of Google.

Contributors

Dr. Rob Mellor – Kingston University, Director of Enterprise, Faculty of Computing, Information Systems and Mathematics

Dr. Anil Hansjee – Google Inc UK, Head of Corporate Development EMEA & Professor of On-Line Knowledge Economy

Mr. Timbo Drayson – Google Inc UK, Product Marketing Manager

Mr. Jonathan Briggs – Professor of eCommerce at Kingston University

Mr. Graham Cooke – Google Inc, UK eCommerce Senior Project Manager

Dr. Souheil Khaddaj – Reader at Kingston University

Resources

Google technology user groups – http://www.gtugs.org. The London one is based at Kingston University. It is basically an attempt by Google to scale up the Google developer days which Google does not have resources for to execute on with all the demand to do these. There is also an external effort to launch a company in 48 hrs which is scaling out to different locations http://www.launch48.com/about/

Code Prize Competitions and other links:

- http://code.google.com/android/adc/
- http://aws.amazon.com/startupchallenge/
- http://www.callingallinnovators.com/default.aspx
- http://www.mobilethisdeveloper.com/#meteor=Wz_6kaYy7vq
- http://www.mashupevent.com/about-mashup
- http://www.cloudcamp.com/?page_id=2
- http://mobilemonday.org.uk/http://www.entrepreneurcountry.net/
- http://www.dreambuildplay.com/main/default.aspx
- http://www.blackberrypartnersfund.com/
- http://www.netflixprize.com/
- http://www.searchmonkeychallenge.com/

And keep looking at http://www.google.com/newproducts

Exercise 2: Calculating benefit

Taylor and Dickens is an old established veterinary practice on the family smallholding in Worcestershire. The vet, Dr Taylor is nearing final retirement (his business partner, Dr Dickens, died some years ago) and together with his semi-retired assistant Mrs Dowdy, runs the office. Dr Taylor has an operating room and takes personal charge of in-house patients. Mrs Dowdy helps him organize a team of 6 veterinary technicians that takes care of most work out-house. The company has been run by the Taylor family for 3 generations, but now the only Taylor left is Dr Taylor's granddaughter, aged 19, who is studying to be an architect. Despite the practice having a very good reputation, business is dropping off as the traditional customers (farms etc.) sell their land to property developers or turn to other sources of income. Dr Taylor had hoped that ponies of wealthy Birmingham families may be a growth area but his expectations have been disappointed. His granddaughter's boyfriend Ken also works for the firm, he retrained as a veterinary technician after a first degree in IT. He keeps on about equipping the roving out-house team with palm-tops not only to better plan their daily route of visits, but also fitting the palm-tops with veterinary diagnostic and reporting software. Mrs Dowdy views their plans to get rid of her ledger-based paper system with utmost distrust. Ken also suggests opening a cattery and kennels where people going on holiday from the nearby midlands airport can drop off their pets while they are away. Ken would also like to have a quarantine unit for incoming animals but he does not know how to go about doing that and despite his enthusiasm there is a vague yet cautious atmosphere around this suggestion, including falling foul of complex regulatory issues.

Describe where Taylor and Dickens are in Knowledge Valley and indicate possible directions. What are the main dangers the organization may encounter?

Annual turnover for Taylor and Dickens is around 500 thousand pounds, varying between 629 thousand pounds on a good year and 252 thousand pound on a lean year. How deep is the tarn of Knowledge Valley for Taylor and Dickens? Using Chapter 14 try to estimate the financial benefits they may accrue as a result of implementing 'best practice' Information Systems.

Exercise 3: An SME

A travel agents decided to start publicizing and selling its products online.

The travel agents specialize in high-end-of-the-market tours; typical customers include many 'gray gold' and other high-earner profiles. Products from this company are very high quality but – despite being offered at 19% markup as opposed to the branch-standard of 33% – the product is still significantly more expensive than cut-price suppliers. Thus the product it offers requires a high information content because it must convince its customers that an e.g. African safari from this supplier is worth the higher price (i.e. in terms of ICDT Theory, it needs a large VTS).

The company is a family-owned SME employing around 120 people, mostly at their HQ, but also at local offices in the major destination areas (Bangkok, Beijing, Cape Town, Mexico and Nairobi). The directors are the owner (a robust 50-year-old technical graduate who is very open to new ideas and technology) supported by his wife (head of marketing) and their best friend (head of new product development). Below this there are 4 sales departments: Orient, Africa, Americas and Adventure Holidays, each with one 'head of *department*'. Salaries are generally low (staff make up for this by travel 'perks') and thus staff churn is high because staff can be attracted to other agents by relatively small pay increases. Bonuses in departments are paid as percentage of salary and are related to whole-company profits (i.e. in a normal year, only heads of departments earn a significant bonus).

The IT department sees its role as being responsible for the IT (esp. hardware) infrastructure, which covers workstations and networks as well as EDI to ticketing gateways (WORLDSPAN, SABRE etc.), but the IT-director is keen to set up web and so on servers in-house. With few exceptions, the IT-ability of the sales staff rarely exceeds computer-driving-license level.

Describe either:

- What you see as the major barriers to the proposed web construction and Internet project.
- The technical system, including any role you may propose for intranet in your scenario.
- Your suggestions towards motivating staff better – possibly in terms of Knowledge Valley Theory.

Exercise 4: Public sector

The Danish Ministry of Agriculture, Fisheries & Food started to streamline its work processes through deploying new IT (especially Internet) technologies.

DMAFF regulates production at farm level (including fishing), through production and processing, to consumer level (publishing hygiene reports on food outlets, as well as food journalism, etc.). Catch, quota and production reporting should be digitalized, reporting on e.g. outbreaks of disease and import/export information is of high importance and duties generally resemble those of Defra in the UK.

Including its inspectors, DMAFF employs around 2400 people, with the largest number – some 500 – concentrated at its HQ. At the HQ, the organization is structured on 3 levels, the management level (director, 2 vice-directors and the heads of departments), the process level (some 450 specialists, mostly graduates, organized into departments) and the support staff (finance, personnel dept., secretaries etc.). Being a political organization, the director can expect to be replaced upon changes of government (approx every 5 years). The other department heads and so on tend to serve much longer terms and have very little mobility. Department heads and so on are on high salaries plus a hefty achievement bonus. Other staff are on nationally agreed pay scales with some minor variations due to personal bonus payments; turnover (churn) among these employees is 23% per annum.

The IT department sees its role as being responsible for the IT (esp. hardware) infrastructure, which is very extensive and covers e.g. all slaughterhouses in the country as well as mobile services to roving inspectors. Internet is regarded as a journalistic tool and is therefore anchored in the PR department. With few exceptions, the IT-ability of the staff working outside the IT department rarely exceeds computer-driving-licence level.

Describe what you see as the major barriers to the proposed project and what measures could be taken to improve performance in terms of Knowledge Valley Theory.

index

task force, 84, 93–95
Taylorism, 27
TCP/IP-based information sharing
    systems, 120
Technology Acceptance Model, 32
Technology Cluster Innovation, 24
Telecommuting, 129
Tesco, 29
Tobins q, 65
TQM, 88, 117
Transaction Cost Theory, 36, 44
the transaction costs for communication,
    20, 28, 123
trans-disciplinarity, 12
trust factor, 11
Turf war, 36

UDDI, 129
U-form organizations, 59
UML, 117, 132
User Generated Content, 123
Utterback, 30, 100

value chain, 38–40, 123
value system, 25, 40, 132

Vertical innovation, 28–31
video-conferencing, 134
Virtual reality, 17, 131
VoIP, 134

watchdog approach, 48
weak ties, 53, 107, 122
Web Ontology Language, 128
Web-based document management, 17,
    135
Wikis, 17, 135
Wisdom of Crowds, 123
Work Light, 130
WSDL, 129

XML, 17, 20, 117, 129
Xoops, 17
X-query, 117

Yahoo, 30
Yahoo Pipes, 130
Yammer, 123
Yellow Pages, 10, 28

Zunft, 13